Counter-Memory, Hope and Aspirations

This book explores the voices of terror-attack survivors, focusing on their experiences of hope and hopelessness, memory and counter-memory, and aspirations and counter aspirations. It establishes linkages between the three to understand how they can be structured into a framework to aid terror survivors.

Focusing on the survivors of the 26/11 Mumbai attacks of 2008, the book explores how hope, memory and aspiration influence healing and resilience. It explores the role that hope, memory and aspirations play in recovery. It looks at the agency of the survivors, public memory and disillusionment, and through narratives of the survivors, presents the struggles they go through in the aftermath of the trauma. The book proposes a new lens for understanding the long-term effects of terror events and the lived realities of those who survive them.

It will be of interest to researchers and academics of disaster management, conflict and conflict resolution, political science and international studies, as well as terror survivor communities. It will also be useful to policy makers and bureaucrats, those working with the rehabilitation of terror survivors.

Jacquleen Joseph is the Professor of Disaster Studies, Centre for Disaster Management, Jamsetji Tata School of Disaster Studies, Tata Institute of Social Sciences, India. She also serves as its current Dean. Her research, field action and teaching at the school are focused on psychosocial care and support in disaster and humanitarian contexts, and her research interests also include disaster risk, vulnerability and recovery in relation to psychosocial well-being.

Surinder K. P. Jaswal is the former Deputy Director (Pro Vice-Chancellor) and Professor of Social Work, Centre for Health and Mental Health, School of Social Work, Tata Institute of Social Sciences, India. She was also the Associate Editor of the *Indian Journal of Social Work* (IJSW). She is a social work educator and public health researcher focusing on inequality and human development issues in health and mental health.

Allan Mathew Alex is a research officer associated with the Jamsetji Tata School of Disaster Studies, Tata Institute of Social Sciences, India. He has engaged in a variety of projects focusing on disaster and trauma recovery, disaster justice and disaster risk in urban development. ORCID 0009-0005-2050-1528

Lavanya Shanbhogue Arvind teaches at the Centre for Disasters and Development, Jamsetji Tata School of Disaster Studies, TISS, India. Her research spans gender and water rights, and disaster studies, with a focus on feminist, intersectional and socially responsive approaches. Her debut novel *The Heavens We Chase* was published in 2016, and her writings have appeared in *HuffPost*, *Hindu Business Line*, *Madras Courier* and *Bloomberg Quint*.

"The Authors bring with them long term experience and expertise in the subject of Disasters of all types. This publication will add to the understanding of the humanitarian aspects of one such terrible event. The serialization of how the human emotions, and the coping mechanism related to such traumatic events in meaningful ways, building resilience".

—**Nimesh G Desai**, *Psychiatrist and Public Health Professional*

"The act of terrorism is inhuman and a devastating pathology for humanity. This book highlights the lived and felt experiences of the survivors of terror attacks from a perspective that shows the internalization of pain and the formation of memory in the personal and public spheres, which are often submerged in the space of time, the nation's priority, and similar other events. The book essentially emphasizes the process and importance of navigating towards building hope, aspirations from the eyes of the survivors of the Mumbai terror attack of 2008".

—**Subhasis Bhadra**, *Professor of Psychiatric Social Work, Head of the Department of Psychosocial Support in Disaster Management, National Institute of Mental Health and Neuro Sciences (NIMHANS), Bengaluru, India.*

"The manuscript will be an asset for the field of disasters as it critically looks at the nature of memorialization over a 10-year period between 2009 and 2019. Further the manuscript will be of immense value for disaster social worker practitioners and educators as it delves into the spatial and emotional significance of memorials, analysing how they function as sites of collective mourning, reflection, and resilience"

—**Ankur Saxena**, *Dean, Department of Social Work, MS Baroda University, Vadodara, Gujarat, India.*

Counter-Memory, Hope and Aspirations

A Case Study of 26/11 Mumbai Terror Attack

Jacquleen Joseph, Surinder K. P. Jaswal, Allan Mathew Alex and Lavanya Shanbhogue Arvind

Routledge
Taylor & Francis Group
LONDON AND NEW YORK

First published 2026
by Routledge
4 Park Square, Milton Park, Abingdon, Oxon OX14 4RN

and by Routledge
605 Third Avenue, New York, NY 10158

Routledge is an imprint of the Taylor & Francis Group, an informa business

British Library Cataloguing-in-Publication Data
A catalogue record for this book is available from the British Library

ISBN: 978-1-032-52054-4 (hbk)
ISBN: 978-1-041-16509-5 (pbk)
ISBN: 978-1-003-68495-4 (ebk)

DOI: 10.4324/9781003684954

Typeset in Times New Roman
by Deanta Global Publishing Services, Chennai, India

To the survivors of terror— whose lives have been irretrievably altered by the unimaginable horror of pain and loss.

Yet you persist, hope, aspire and remember even when the world forgets.

This work is for you.

Contents

Preface

This work emerges from the Field Action Project by the Tata Institute of Social Sciences (TISS) and the Taj Public Service Welfare Trust (TPSWT) as a response to the 26/11 Mumbai terror attack in 2008 that later extended to centrifugal disasters such as the 13/7 Mumbai triple bomb blasts in 2011 and the 9/12 Kolkata AMRI hospital fire in 2011. The Field Action Project has documented the unique needs and concerns of the survivors and their recovery trajectories. Helmed by Professor Jacquleen Joseph, senior faculty member at JTSDS, and Professor Surinder K. P. Jaswal, the then Deputy Director of TISS, this project titled "An Avenue for Psychosocial and Therapeutic Interventions" has developed and tested customized theoretical models of response and advocated for appropriate policy change. Over the years, a rights-based and survivor-centric approach coupled with integrated recovery and psychosocial interventions has helped address the issues of pathologizing, dehumanization, control and de-politicization of the survivors.

This work emerges from a need to examine and document how individuals and communities reconstruct their lives after terror. The high-decibel public discourse, acts of remembering and processes of memorialization shape public memory and veers it towards nationalistic fervour and jingoism. Yet, what largely remains unrecognised and relegated to the margins are the lived and felt experiences of survivors and their families. Traversing interdisciplinary inquiries from the social sciences, psychology, trauma studies, memory studies and disaster recovery, the various chapters in this book conceptually explore hope, aspiration, hopelessness, official and public memory, counter-memory and aspirations, distress, anger and grief as remembered by survivors themselves.

Drawing from survivor voices and narratives, this work demonstrates the invisibility of survivorship; while survivors carry the weight of loss, remembrance, daily endurance and survival itself, their voices are missing in official narratives.

The five chapters in this volume traverse the nature of survivor invisibility, memory, hope, aspiration, counter narratives and recovery. The chapters explore how the politics of space, public memorials and official acts of remembrance simultaneously perform acts of commemoration and erasure. The emergence of hopelessness, counter-memory and aspirations reflects subtle acts of subversion by survivors.

The final chapter critiques the disciplinary gaps and social exclusions that often place survivors in a position where they become legally unrecognized, emotionally unsupported and socially available as a nonentity. It defends the need to pay attention to the silences as much as voices of the survivors' realities while calling for renewed attention focused on scholarly and policy interventions.

It is hoped that this volume will create new possibilities of framing questions of memory, aspiration and recovery through powerful narratives and voices of those most affected.

Foreword

It is with delight (and some trepidation) that I accepted Surinder's request to write a foreword to this book. Surinder is not only a friend but also someone I have admired for a long time because of her mental health scholarship over the past three decades. I was fearful due to my complete inexperience with this task, having never done it before.

I always wonder if book readers bother to read a foreword. To me, book forewords are included due to historical habit, rather than serving an actual purpose. As a reader, I confess to skipping forewords and getting to the main course directly. So, what exactly is the purpose of a foreword, really?

Gemini, the AI-driven version of Google (there, I brought in something very topical), tells me a foreword is "to provide credibility and endorsement to the book and its author by someone other than the author. It often introduces the book to readers, highlighting its significance and why they should read it". Let's see if I can rise to the task.

This is a book about the survivors of the 26/11 terror attacks in Mumbai. It is the culmination of a 10-year mental health intervention with the survivors and their families. It may seem that a book about events that happened 17 years ago is a bit dated and that the world has moved on, but this book is a reminder that this is not true for survivors and their families. For them, the trauma in the aftermath of an event where they were unwilling and unexpected participants continues even with the passage of time. Everyone remembers the victims, but the mental health impact on survivors and families is forgotten as society gathers the pieces and focuses on the future.

This is true not just about public disasters such as terrorism (or floods, for example) but also about private disasters – the survivors of suicide. We have little to no psychosocial support in India for survivors of both types of disasters. This book is a welcome addition to improve our understanding of the mental health needs of survivors and an example of praxis to support survivors over time. This book plays a valuable role in identifying key gaps in our current understanding and practice, illustrated by the lived and felt experiences of survivors. The authors draw our attention to the problem of valorising the agency of survivors fuelled by hope and resilience, against a background of institutional and policy indifference resulting in negligible recovery support services.

This book also highlights an important unsavoury aspect of public memory of terrorism events – the marginalization of survivors. Their current lives in a post-event world are relegated to the margins, and their struggles are transformed into tokenistic imagery to provoke jingoism.

The studies described in this book highlight a range of research methods, strategies and data sources which can be used to ascertain practical solutions for the marginalization of survivors. The use of a life course research design allows for an in-depth engagement with the lived and felt experiences of the survivors over a prolonged period of time.

The authors interrogate the intersections of memory, memorials and monuments, exploring the tension between official memory – often state-sanctioned – and counter-memory, which challenges dominant narratives. The authors examine how these competing forces shape the process of public remembering, influencing not just historical consciousness but also policy, practice and public sentiment.

The counter aspirations emerging from survivor narratives chart the way forward for shaping praxis and policy in the Global South, where memorials, therapeutic and support services are largely unavailable. This is invaluable for students, researchers and policy makers in India and the Global South as they grapple with the challenge of addressing survivor needs empathetically in resource-constrained settings.

If this has whetted your appetite, now is a good time to grab a cup of tea (or coffee, depending on your choice of poison) and a quiet corner to turn the page over and jump headlong into the first chapter of the book. I hope you enjoy the experience, and the book leaves you with practical insights you can use in the future.

Soumitra Pathare MD, MRCPsych, PhD
Director
Centre for Mental Health Law and Policy
Indian Law Society
Pune, India
May 2025

Abbreviations

AAPTI	An Avenue for Psychosocial and Therapeutic Interventions
AWWA	Amputees and War Wounded Association
BJP	Bharatiya Janata Party
CAG	Comptroller and Auditor General of India
CBT	Cognitive Behavioural Therapy (CBT)
CPT	Cognitive Processing Therapy (CPT)
CrPC	Code of Criminal Procedure
CST	Chhatrapati Shivaji Terminus
DBT	Dialectical Behaviour Therapy (DBT)
DRR	Disaster Risk Reduction
DSM	Diagnostic and Statistical Manual of Mental Disorder
ECOSOC	Economic and Social Council of the United Nations
EMDR	Eye Movement Desensitization and Reprocessing
ETA	Euskadi Ta Askatasuna
FBI	Federal Bureau of Investigation
FIA	Federal Investigation Agency
GRP	Government Railway Police
GTD	Global Terrorism Database
IAS	Indian Administrative Service
INC	Indian National Congress
INR	Indian Rupee
IPC	Indian Penal Code
ISI	Inter-Services Intelligence, Pakistan
JTSDS	Jamsetji Tata School of Disaster Studies
JuD	Jamaat ud Dawa
LeT	Lashkar-e-Taiba
MHA	Ministry of Home Affairs
NARM	Neuro Affective Relational Model
NCSMS	National Committee for Strengthening Maritime and Coastal Security
NDA	National Democratic Alliance
NGO	Non-Governmental Organization

NIA	National Investigation Agency
NSG	National Security Guards (NSGs)
PFA	Psychosocial First Aid
POTA	Prevention of Terrorism Act (POTA)
PTSD	Post-Traumatic Stress Disorder
RPF	Railway Protection Force (RPF)
SATP	South Asian Terrorism Database
START	National Consortium for the Study of Terrorism and Responses to Terrorism
TADA	Terrorism and Disruptive Activities Act 1985
TPSWT	Taj Public Service Welfare Trust (TPSWT)
TISS	Tata Institute of Social Science
UAPA	The Unlawful Activities (Prevention) Act 1967, Unlawful Activities (Prevention) Amendment Act, 2008
UNOCT	United Nations Office of Counter Terrorism
UPA	United Progressive Alliance
VT	Victoria Terminus
WHO	World Health Organization
WTC	World Trade Centre

1 The Invisible Survivors of Terror

Terrorism is an extensively studied subject across the world. Since the attack on the World Trade Center on 11 September 2001, studies on the actors and their motivations for terrorism have shifted from the previous century. Duyvesteyn (2004) speaks of how these studies describe the current form of terrorism as something 'new' and go on to explore this 'new' form of terrorism. She argues that terrorism has not undergone any significant changes. While the actors and their ideals may be different, ultimately their actions differ little.

However, despite these misgivings, terrorism has resulted in the rise of new fields of study such as terrorism studies. This field broke off from counter-insurgency studies into a separate niche in the 1970s, consisting of leading scholars and situating itself as an important but small field at the edges of security studies and international relations (Jackson, 2012). This field remained on the fringes well into the 1980s and 1990s but erupted into a massive and critical field in the 21st century, primarily due to the 11 September 2001 attacks on the World Trade Centre (Jackson, 2012). This growth has been characterized by dedicated terrorism scholars and an influx of funding which has led to collaborative efforts with other fields, adding a multi-disciplinary flavour. The multi-disciplinary turn of terrorism studies has resulted in an epistemological pluralization alongside an exploration of topics previously understudied in terrorism studies such as gender and terrorism, amongst others (Jackson, 2012). Thus, in the 21st century, terrorism studies have developed into a critical field that has been diversified and nurtured through multi-disciplinary focus and efforts. Unfortunately, this growth does not imply that terrorism studies have managed to adequately spread its focus to all the research areas within terrorism studies that require it.

The overemphasis on certain issues and marginal attention paid to others has skewed the focus of terrorism studies. Topics such as radicalization, weapons of mass destruction terrorism, Islamist terrorism are examples of topics that are the focus of the ever-expanding purview of terrorism literature (Jackson, 2012). On the other hand, topics such as the history of terrorism, evaluation of counter-terrorism measures and terrorism in the Global South

DOI: 10.4324/9781003684954-1

have gained far less of a research focus (Jackson, 2012). The focus on certain research areas is a result of the Western influence on terrorism studies, and this influence, shaped by Western understandings and agendas, has limited the scope of terrorism studies. Critical terrorism studies emerged as a field to address some of these concerns and, in its wake has critiqued policies and practices, such as counter-terrorism policies, that are in violation of human rights, threat to democracy and contribute to the 'terrorist othering' of certain communities (McGowan, 2016). However, despite these advances by critical terrorism studies to address some of the failings of terrorism studies, it has still fallen short of bringing focus to a significantly understudied group in terrorism studies: the survivors of terrorism (McGowan, 2016).

At present, terror survivors have been relegated to politicized, sympathetic beings that are used to justify and propel aggressive counter-terrorism policies (McGowan, 2016). Furthermore, the survivors who challenge mainstream political discourses on terrorism are often disregarded and denied opportunities to reshape these discourses (McGowan, 2016). This results in paternalistic policies and attitudes being adopted by the state towards terror survivors with little regard for their personal experiences with terrorism.

Such attitudes and policies often portray terror survivors as dependants who need help, be it materially and/or psychologically. While these do bring out the needs of the survivors, they tend to downplay their agency. Every terror survivor is an individual with their own hopes, aspirations and much more. However, their identities are often reduced to that of a victim, and their hopes and aspirations are often abandoned due to trauma and injury. Furthermore, the trauma and injury are compounded by institutional indifference, as mainstream political discourse rarely takes into account what the survivors need in the aftermath of a terror event. When considering this reality, it is imperative that we consider the agency and the voices of the survivors in shaping policies and discourses that affect them. As a first step, this study has chosen to use the term "survivor" rather than "victim" to highlight those affected by terror events. The use of these terms is highly contentious and politicized (McGowan, 2016). Nevertheless, this study seeks to use the term "survivor" rather than "victim" to describe the communities that continue to live on in the aftermath of terrorism. The distinction and reasoning behind this are as follows.

"Victims of terrorism" does not have an agreed upon international definition (UNOCT et al., 2022). Despite this, agencies such as the United Nations have defined, for those affected by terror events, actions based on human rights and humanitarian frameworks as well as counter-terrorism treaties and conventions (UNOCT et al., 2022). However, these actions tend to focus on recognition, protection and compensation. Member States are encouraged to act to protect the security of their nations and address the needs of the victims. Finally, while the voices of victims are encouraged to be heard, this is primarily to counter terrorist narratives. While there is some conversation on long-term rehabilitation, there is little conversation on what that means for the victims of terrorism (UNOCT et al., 2022). These conceptualizations of victims at an international level have revealed that a victim is defined on the basis of the event. This results in the invisibilization of their lives before and after the event. The injustice and suffering they face because of an ill-equipped system, poor memorialization processes and apathy from the general public are overlooked as the terror event and terrorists become the focus. Due to these associations of the term "victim", this study chose the term "survivor" to refer to people who 'live on' beyond the event. However, the term "victim" is not entirely omitted; instead, it is used to refer to people who lost their lives to terror events and in reference to policies, laws, newspaper articles and other documents which use the term as a descriptor.

Most definitions of the term "survivor" define it as "a person who continues to live after an accident, illness, war, etc". This is an important distinction from the term "victim". While the term "victim" tends to be defined around the event and therefore actions are focused on countering and recovering from the event, the term "survivor" is associated with living. This includes their lives before the event, their experiences during the event and their lives after the event. It is important to examine the lives of the survivors across the spectrum, as it enables one to understand the injustices and suffering they face throughout their lives, not just due to the event but also due to the policy environment and the systems that continue to reject their appeals for justice. Thus, the term "survivor" in this study is used to highlight that, while the event is a significant moment that has altered their lives forever, the lives of the survivors and their lived experiences are far more relevant to understanding needs and demands for justice. Thus, rather than having the event define them, we seek to have the survivors' lives define them.

Thus it is crucial to identify the survivors of terror events, specifically the worst impacted survivors. There have been several terror incidents in the 21st century. However, there is little talk of who has been the worst impacted by the terror events. Terror events often result in prolonged disruption of the everyday lives of the survivors. In identifying the worst impacted survivors, one understands who needs the most help and, in turn, the best means by which resources can be best utilized to allow those who have had their lives shattered to begin a process of picking up the pieces and getting back on their feet.

During the course of the study, two secondary databases were identified and studied. The first is the Global Terrorism Database (GTD), which compiles data at an international level. This database has been compiled and maintained by the National Consortium for the Study of Terrorism and Responses to Terrorism (START) at the University of Maryland since 2006, along with the GTD: Codebook, Methodology, Inclusion Criteria and Variables Descriptions (2021). The second database is the South Asia Terrorism Portal (SATP), which was set up and maintained by the Institute for Conflict Management based in New Delhi (South Asia Terrorism Portal, n.d.). These databases enable us to closely examine the on-ground reality of the impacts of terrorism.

The first dataset to be examined is one pertaining to terror attacks across regions in the world. Upon examination of the numbers from 2010–2018, the conclusion arrived at is that the three worst affected regions are the Middle Eastern and North African region, the South Asian region and the Sub-Saharan African region. If one were to look at the worst affected countries according to the database in the same time period, it is seen that nearly 95% of these countries belong to these three regions. While this is no surprise, it is of concern that India, the focus of this study, is part of this list with a death toll of 3,114 over a period of 8 years from 2010 to 2018. Within India, the worst affected region, since the turn of the 21st century, excluding Jammu, Kashmir, Punjab and the Northeast, is the state of Maharashtra, with the city of Mumbai recording 11 of the total 17 incidents that have taken place in the state. This paints Mumbai as a soft terror target, especially due to its symbolic value as the financial capital of the country (for more information, refer to https://youtu.be/SBrH4F_KoeQ).

It is important to understand who is affected and who exactly suffers when such (terror) attacks take place. If one were to view the scenario on a global scale, it would be evident that civilians are the ones who suffer the worst ill effects of terror attacks, followed by security forces, often considered martyrs, while government officials and politicians are the least affected. It is pertinent to keep in mind that the civilian list is exempt from attacks on journalists, tourists, educational institutions and religious institutions. Despite this, civilians have dominated the list of casualties. A look at the statistics shows a similar trend prevalent in India too. In India, civilian losses far exceed the losses sustained by the security forces and government officials and politicians. This is despite the numbers being only for the period of 2010–2018 which omits events such as the 26/11 Mumbai terror attack of 2008.

Another aspect to keep in mind is the fact that these databases do not contain information about survivors. These numbers (of survivors) would far outweigh the casualties, as they include family members who were dependent on the deceased and the permanently disabled. These numbers are vital to adequately plan interventions and distribute resources so that those who are the most severely affected receive help to recover and move forward with their lives.

Last but not least, there is a need to understand the on-ground scenario considering this information. What are the provisions for victims and survivors, considering that civilians are the worst affected? What is the place for victims and survivors within public memory? Are they remembered or forgotten over time? How does this remembering/forgetting affect the psychological well-being of survivors? At present, terrorism studies do not sufficiently explore the answers to these questions.

Since terrorism studies and critical terrorism studies have done little work with terror survivors, the current study looked at trauma studies to understand if there was work done with terror survivors, especially around the above questions. Work with terror survivors, to date, has primarily focused on Post-Traumatic Stress Disorder (PTSD), in relation to the terror event. This is because discourse and research on trauma surrounding terrorism often emerge from within Western academic settings. This discourse and research are shaped by Western cultural frames that are rooted in positivist thinking and individualism (Bracken, 2002; Brown, 2017). Social and cultural factors are often regarded as secondary factors that can influence individual trauma but are never treated as the primary framework to understand the persistence of trauma in individuals and how they navigate their trauma (Bracken, 2002). Furthermore, the meaning-making process is often associated with restructuring individual schemas that have been shattered due to trauma (Dalenberg et al., 2017). Such an understanding neglects how social and cultural contexts influence the formation of world views over the course of an individual's life, how trauma itself is a function of these social and cultural contexts and how meaning-making is shaped in the aftermath by these contexts. This results in the Western individual trauma care model often failing in non-Western settings that do not adhere to such an individualistic social and cultural settings (Bracken, 2002).

Coupled with these issues is the problematic view of trauma being associated primarily with the traumatic event (Bracken, 2002). While Dalenberg et al. (2017) points out the problematic nature of defining trauma in relation to certain qualifying events that are assessed as "threatening" or "aversive", they do not question why trauma is associated so closely with just the event. Regher and Gutheil (2002) point out how the judicial process associated with punishing a crime can serve to hinder the healing process for victims. When considering this, there emerges a need to understand if institutional processes associated with compensation, familial structures and public apathy become traumatic experiences. Thus, this study seeks to move beyond associating trauma simply with the event and seeks to capture the pre- and post-event experiences and examine them as possible contributors to survivors' trauma.

This brings us to the next issue currently present in Western individual trauma care models: the fixation on therapeutic processes. Therapeutic processes seek to focus on individual healing and neglect issues of injustice. Furthermore, they tend to focus on concepts such as positive growth and positive emotions such as hope and joy, and they tend to dismiss anger and hopelessness as negative traits or pathological processes (Morland et al., 2008). These views neglect the power of anger and hopelessness to unite people who have suffered injustices and resist structures that have contributed to their suffering in the aftermath of a traumatic event. Furthermore, critical psychology points out that these interventions emerge from a Western individualized setting and often place the onus of recovery on the survivors (Brown,

2017). Furthermore, a universal categorization of "traumatic events" and their symptoms is a fixation for the positivist-influenced model of Western psychotherapy. The criticisms by Dalenberg et al (2017) of definitions of trauma that focus on individual meaning-making (of trauma), as not lending towards the development of general worldwide or regionwide lists of traumatic events, illustrate the same. Such criticisms once again dismiss the influence of social and cultural contexts in shaping how an individual and community experience trauma. While this is a criticism of trauma studies in general, further examination of studies that specifically explore the trauma of terrorism reveals similar failings.

Trauma studies on terror survivors, which emerged in the aftermath of 9/11, tend to focus on PTSD in the aftermath of the terror event, whilst largely ignoring the social and cultural contexts within which the terror event and the trauma associated with it have occurred (Durodié & Wainwright, 2019). Furthermore, the PTSD approach to studying the trauma of terrorism has led to the pathologization of emotions such as anger, in order to identify them as markers of post-traumatic stress (Durodié & Wainwright, 2019). Such an act renders normal emotional responses to such harrowing experiences as markers of disease and therefore in need of treatment. This is dangerous as it can allow for survivors and their demands to be dismissed as being the result of PTSD and deepen the state's paternalistic approach. PTSD-based approaches to the trauma of terrorism tend to focus on the terror event and its impact on terror survivors (Durodié & Wainwright, 2019) and seldom question the institutional structures that contribute to their suffering in the time beyond the event. Whilst PTSD is certainly an important area of research when considering terror survivors, an overindulgence in PTSD has led to other aspects such as structural violence, public apathy, inadequate memorialization processes and their relation to the trauma of terrorism being severely understudied, especially in the long-term lives of terror survivors.

To depart from the PTSD and event-centric nature of terrorism trauma studies, this study takes up two ontological positions based on Heidegger's concept of *Dasein* (Bracken, 2002). Firstly, the study shifts away from the ontological dualism, courtesy of Descartes, that informs trauma studies in general. Ontological dualism tends to separate the mind and the world and therefore sees the mind as an entity separate from the world (Bracken, 2002). This results in social and cultural contexts, within which traumatic events occur, being deemed unnecessary to address trauma in individuals. This perspective allows for therapeutic approaches to be the dominant frame to study and address trauma, as it disregards context and sees trauma as an individualistic response to a traumatic event which can be treated. Moving away from this, the study takes the ontological position of human beings being situated within the world through social and cultural structures (Bracken, 2002). The world and the human being, therefore, simultaneously affect and are affected by each other and are inseparable.

Secondly, most PTSD studies take up a linear position on time from pre-event to event to post-event; however, such a linear conception does not allow for an adequate understanding of the trauma suffered by the survivors and the sense-making process that survivors engage with to understand their trauma (Bracken, 2002). Therefore, it is necessary to engage with the past, present and future simultaneously. Thus, the study rejects the event-centric approach of PTSD studies in favour of an ontological frame based on a non-linear engagement with time, to understand the trauma and the sense-making process of the survivors.

Based on these ontological positions, the study engages with memory, hope/hopelessness, aspirations and lived and felt experiences as the epistemological conduits to understand the trauma and injuries felt and experienced by terror survivors. These concepts were selected due to their ability to capture the social and cultural contexts of the survivors, their close conceptual links with each other and with survivor agency and identity (the most dominant social and cultural dimensions explored in terror studies). Furthermore, the temporal dimension inherent within these concepts satisfies the non-linear temporal dimension specified by the ontological position of the study.

Memory and lived and felt experiences serve as the foundation and approach respectively, for the concepts explored within this study. Survivor memory allows for insight into the personal experiences and rationales of the survivors, enabling us to understand the deeply embedded foundation behind their trauma, injury and recovery. In addition, engagement with collective memory allows for immersion into the processes of remembrance, such as rationalizing the terror event, memorialization, official memory and counter-memory; the means by which they are formed, the reasons for their emergence and the role they play in exacerbating or ameliorating trauma and injury. Finally, memory exists in the past, present and future (Brockmeier, 2002). It is shaped by a world which is historical and constantly evolving (Brockmeier, 2002; Bracken, 2002), allowing for memory to exist not as an account of the past, but as a temporally and contextually shaped element, allowing for a non-linear view of trauma when viewed alongside the context.

Therefore, memory cannot be studied in isolation from context. Memory is shaped, retained, restructured and forgotten based on the social and cultural frames (Brockmeier, 2002; Olfason 1987, as cited in Bracken, 2002). Furthermore, memories are associated with human relations, complicated feelings and emotions, and disregarding these would undercut the meaning behind the memories and the complex processes related to their formation. Towards this, lived and felt experiences serve as a crucial approach in capturing the context for memories and understanding why survivors choose to remember, forget or reshape their memories.

With memories and lived and felt experiences serving as foundation – context, hope/hopelessness and aspirations provide the means for understanding the needs, wants, actions and agency of the survivors. The ontological position dictates a co-affective relationship between the human and the world. Hope/hopelessness and aspirations serve as the means for realizing this relationship. Hope has been categorized as a force for initiating action (Freire, 1994) and an aspirational capacity (Appadurai, 2004). However, this study looks at hope as a biotechnology (Wrangel, 2019) and has a deeper interest in the shattering of hope which leads to disillusionment and hopelessness. This allows us to evaluate emotions such as anger and sorrow not as negative feelings which need to be 'corrected', but as essential feelings which allow for action and agency. Aspirations play a similar role in the study. The transformation of aspirations over time due to the complex entanglement of disillusionment, memories and lived and felt experiences alongside the disconnect with state-proposed aspirations is crucial to understanding how and why survivors take up action.

In summary, the linkages between memories, hope/hopelessness, aspirations and lived and felt experiences have the potential to capture the intricate experience, context and nature of trauma, injury and recovery. This allows the study to adopt an epistemological framework based on ontological positions in opposition to mainstream PTSD and event-centric studies. The AAPTI (An Avenue for Psychosocial and Therapeutic Interventions) project, the empirical foundation of this study, was co-affective in developing this frame of thought.

The AAPTI model emerged as a response to gaps in intervention following the 26/11 Mumbai terror attacks in 2008 in India. The then-present traumatic stress-informed models for intervention provided little assistance for the long-term recovery of the terror survivors in the Global South context. These interventions focused on emergency health services and ex gratia payments as being sufficient to aid the recovery of survivors, with little regard for pre-existing socio-structural constraints, vulnerabilities and long-term and intergenerational trauma. To address this, AAPTI was conceived. It evolved to provide long-term assistance and interventions for the most vulnerable families in the aftermath of the 26/11 attack. This was phase I of the project. It has since extended towards interventions in other disasters during phases II and III, such as the 13 July 2011 Mumbai Triple Blast and 9 December 2001 Kolkata Hospital Fire. AAPTI focused on understanding the struggles of the survivors and their recovery, developing context-based interventions, building support networks and engaging in policy advocacy. These interventions were grounded in the ontological position and epistemological concepts presented above and contributed to further elaborating on understanding the psychological distress among survivors. As a result of this grounding, AAPTI was able to contextualize the distress of survivors within their socio-structural location, lived and felt experiences, hope/hopelessness and aspirations. Thus, AAPTI represents a praxis based on the alternative ontological and epistemological location presented above, providing empirical grounding for the alternative model for addressing psychological distress in the Global South.

This book is thus based on the findings from AAPTI and lies at an intersection between critical terrorism studies and trauma studies. It contributes to improving the currently lacking space of survivor-related studies in critical terrorism whilst calling for new methodological and ontological approaches to studying the trauma of terrorism as well as trauma in general. With the study and its undertaking established, the content of the chapters is presented below.

Chapter 2 elaborates on the themes through which the selected terror event is studied. These themes include memory, hope and aspirations. The important role of memory and counter-memory in aiding the survivors' recovery, as well as its ties to both justice and democracy, is discussed in depth here. Then we look at hope and disillusionment and the role they play in the survivors' engagement with the event and the state. Finally, we examine the concept of aspirations and how it evolves with the survivors' circumstances.

Chapter 3 looks at the terror event known as the 26/11 attack that happened in the city of Mumbai on 26 November 2008. This event was chosen due to its widespread recognition and its location in a city in the Global South, a geography that is understudied in terrorism studies. This allowed us to look at surrounding narratives and discourses that have informed the official memory of the event. Once the official memory is understood, it helped us understand how the memorialization had come about and what is acknowledged in the memorials and anniversaries. Furthermore, it deals with the memorialization that occurred after the event. However, we also look at memorialization in India outside of 26/11. We have a few examples of terror events in 21st-century India and how these memorialization events vary significantly from the 26/11 memorial event. The problems with the memorialization of terror events are discussed here.

Chapter 4 elaborates on the empirical foundations of the theoretical perspective that has evolved from this study. Through the voices of the survivors, the exploration of governmental practices and narratives brings forward the interlinkages between memory, hope, hopelessness and aspirations. This interlinkage lies at the core of the theoretical perspective that also explores counter-memory and counter-aspirations that emerge from the core concepts of memory, hope and aspirations.

Chapter 5, the concluding chapter, summarizes the findings of the study and how they can be useful in aiding the survivors to engage in a recovery process that respects their right to dignity and does not simply reduce them to "victims" of the event that need support. It highlights the emerging theoretical and practical understandings in the study around trauma, memory, aspirations, agency and recovery for terror survivors and the contributions of the study to these fields of study.

References

Appadurai, A. (2004). The capacity to aspire: Culture and the terms of recognition. In V. Rao & M. Walton (Eds.), *Culture and public action* (pp. 59–94). Stanford University Press.

Bracken, P. (2002). *Trauma: Culture, meaning and philosophy*. Whurr Publishers.

Brockmeier, J. (2002). Remembering and forgetting: Narrative as cultural memory. *Culture & Psychology*, *8*(1), 15–43.

Brown, L. S. (2017). Contributions of feminist and critical psychologies to trauma psychology. In S. N. Gold (Ed.), *APA handbook of trauma psychology* (pp. 501–525). American Psychological Association.

Dalenberg, C. J., Straus, E., & Carlson, E. B. (2017). Defining trauma. In S. N. Gold (Ed.), *APA Handbook of Trauma Psychology* (pp. 15–33). American Psychological Association.

Durodié, B., & Wainwright, D. (2019). Terrorism and post-traumatic stress disorder: A historical review. *The Lancet Psychiatry*, *6*(1), 61–71.

Duyvesteyn, I. (2004). How new is the new terrorism? *Studies in Conflict & Terrorism*, *27*(5), 439–454.

Freire, P. (1994). *Pedagogy of hope: Reliving pedagogy of the oppressed*. Continuum.

Jackson, R. (2012). The study of terrorism 10 years after 9/11: Successes, issues, challenges. *Uluslararası İlişkiler Dergisi*, *8*(32), 1–16.

McGowan, W. (2016). Critical terrorism studies, victimisation, and policy relevance: compromising politics or challenging hegemony?. *CRITICAL STUDIES*, *9*(1), 12-32.

Morland, L. A., Butler, L. D., & Leskin, G. A. (2008). Resilience and thriving in a time of terrorism. In S. Joseph & P. A. Linley (Eds.), *Trauma, recovery, and growth positive psychological perspectives on posttraumatic stress* (pp. 39–61). Wiley-Blackwell.

Regehr, C., & Gutheil, T. (2002). Apology, justice, and trauma recovery. *Journal of the American Academy of Psychiatry and the Law Online*, *30*(3), 425.

South Asia Terrorism Portal. (n.d.). Datasheet. https://www.satp.org/

United Nations Office of Counter Terrorism (UNOCT), the Inter-Parliamentary Union (IPU), & United Nations Office on Drugs and Crime (UNODC). (2022). Model legislative provisions: To support the needs and protect the rights of victims of terrorism. https://www.unodc.org/documents/terrorism/Website2021/220204_model_legislative_provisions.pdf

University of Maryland. (2021). *GTD: Codebook: Methodology, inclusion criteria, and variables*. https://www.start.umd.edu/sites/default/files/2024-10/Codebook.pdf

Wrangel, C. T. (2019). Biopolitics of hope and security: Governing the future through US counterterrorism communications. *Globalizations*, *16*(5), 664–677.

2 Memory, Hope and Aspiration

Drawing from Heidegger (Bracken, 2002), the study shifts from the ontological dualism of mind vs world and conceives human beings as situated within the world through social and cultural structures, wherein the two (mind and world) are conceptualized as co-affected and co-constituted. The ontological position chosen also distances itself from the linear position on time from pre-event to post-event or the event-centric approach, to embrace the non-linear engagement with time, to understand the situatedness of trauma and the sense-making process of the survivors. Grounded in these ontological positions, the study engages with memory, hope/hopelessness, aspirations and lived and felt experiences as the epistemological conduits to understand the situated trauma and the injuries experienced and felt by terror survivors. Memory and lived and felt experiences serve as the foundation and approach respectively for the concepts explored within this study. As memories are closely associated with human relations, complicated feelings and emotions, they are dynamically shaped, forgotten, retained and restructured by the changing social and cultural frames. Thus, memory cannot be studied in isolation of context. Towards this, lived and felt experiences serve as a crucial approach in capturing the context for memories and understanding why survivors choose to remember, forget or reshape their memories. With memories and lived and felt experiences serving as foundation and context, hope/hopelessness and aspirations provide the means for understanding the needs, wants, actions and agency of the survivors. The ontological position dictates a co-affective relationship between the human and the world. Hope/hopelessness and aspirations serve as the means for realizing this relationship. In the sub-sections below, we attempt to understand what we already know from existing literature about memory, hope/hopelessness and aspirations (in line with the alternative ontological position), the gaps in our understanding and how the study was conceptualized to make a beginning contribution to the body of knowledge on trauma and memory.

DOI: 10.4324/9781003684954-2

Social Science Conception of Memory

When viewed in the context of terror events, memory provides historical continuity from before the event to life after the event. But what exactly does memory constitute? Is it simply the idea of not forgetting, or is it more than just remembering and forgetting? Brockmeier (2002) states how remembering is often associated with a positive effect, while forgetting, which results in a loss or an emptiness, is often associated with a negative effect. However, the ability to forget and reshape memories is an important part of alternative conceptions of recovery like social repair, as it allows communities and individuals to work on their memories to enable themselves to heal and repair after harrowing experiences like disasters and terrorism.

Brockmeier (2002) speaks of the culture of remembering and forgetting and the renewed importance of memory in the modern and post-modern capitalist society. This work is especially relevant for looking at terror events in urban localities, where such events mostly tend to happen (Crenshaw, 1981; Beall, 2007). Urban localities are the epitome of a capitalist society. The constant change of modernity is best experienced in the hubbub of cities. Before stepping into the importance of memory in capitalist societies, it is important to understand the culture of remembering and forgetting as described by Brockmeier (2002).

Remembering is an important practice in modern society. From independence days to the birthdays of national heroes, our society fixates on what Brockmeier (2002) describes a "culture of anniversaries". These forms of public commemoration vary from public gatherings like ceremonies to artefacts like books and, most importantly symbolic structures like monuments (2002). With such widespread efforts directed towards remembrance, it is important to understand that these efforts are made to connect societies through two dimensions: social and temporal. These dimensions create a symbolic space of meaning that allows individuals to bond together as well as to be connected across generations (2002). Shared memory of a similarly shared past, along with shared societal values and rules, results in a worldview that acts as a connective tissue that binds people together. This creates a culture of belonging different from, say, race, kinship etc. The temporal dimension of memory allows for the past, present and future to exist together in memory as memory allows one to reminisce about the past while living in the present and gazing upon the future. This aspect of memory is key in its ability to generate and propagate another important agentic force, which is hope as well as hopelessness. This will be elaborated upon in the subsequent section on hope. Now it is important to see modern society's association with memory.

Traditional societies do not undergo constant change, and their need to preserve memories is thus minimal. Capitalist societies, on the other hand, characterized best by cities, undergo constant change. With constant innovations, competition and the need to stay afloat and survive, both organizations and individuals are constantly on the move and trying to stay "modern" to ensure their survival in this society. As a consequence, even the most horrific events are forgotten quickly. This invites a "memory crisis", as pointed out by various authors (e.g., Assmann, 1992; Gross, 2000; Terdiman, 1993) in modern society. This "memory crisis" causes a need to look at not just the process of memory (i.e., the storage process); it also requires a look at the content of memory (what is remembered?) (Brockmeier, 2002). This is influenced by the cultural context such as culture specific values. This ushers in the idea of selective remembering, which blurs the line between remembering and forgetting.

> Since Bartlett, Vygotsky and Luria, psychological researchers of memory have brought forward a number of arguments that human memorizing and remembering cannot be properly understood without taking into account the social functions it fulfills and the cultural web in which it is integrated.
>
> (Brockmeier, 2002, p. 21)

This understanding allows us to look at remembering and forgetting, not as antagonistic to each other but instead as parts of the process of memorization. Therefore, public memory and public amnesia are shaped by what is chosen to be remembered, who is chosen to be remembered and how the public chooses to remember the event. This selective nature of memory is used by nations to legitimize their claims, actions, power and institutions (Rasmussen, 2002).

Memory is communicated to the public through three forms: linguistic, semiotic and performative or discursive (Brockmeier, 2002). Linguistic narrative makes use of oral narratives to spread the memory. In this case, the words and the elements of the story being told, such as the description of the case and historical and political background, create a complex plot that is conveyed to the populace. In the semiotic narrative, it is the symbolism that provides meaning. This memory is informed by the meaning that is provided by structures and symbols surrounding a particular event. Finally, the discursive or performative order argues that what is being narrated is not as important as how it is being narrated. In this case, the local context becomes exceedingly important. This is because, depending on the local context, the narration will vary significantly, and thus elements being portrayed will vary. Thus, the primary objective of a performative narrative is to 'position' the viewers to take a certain perspective towards an event.

All these factors regarding memory set the foundation for memorialization after horrific events. In her work, *Terrorism and Collective Memories: Comparing Bologna, Naples and Madrid 11 March*, Tota (2005) compares memorialization activities across three different terror events in Italy and Spain.

Tota (2005) ties memory to the very essence of democracy. Since official memories of events are often recorded and perpetuated by the government, it becomes essential that this memorialization is done faithfully. This is because memorialization plays a significant role in justice for the survivors. If the event is remembered and not forgotten, it serves as a reminder that there are those who are still awaiting justice. Conveniently forgetting or selectively remembering certain parts of the event will result in people forming a counter-memory that is against the "official" memory of the event. These counter-memories often accuse the powers that be of rigging the system against the survivors or, in some cases (state terror or state inaction against perpetrators), accuse the government of planning and executing the event. These counter-memories may end up being the public memory of the event as opposed to the "official" memory.

In her comparison of the three events, Tota (2005) makes the following arguments. The memorial at Bologna is termed a case of "perfect remembering". On 2nd August 1980, a bomb exploded at the Bologna Railway Station, resulting in 85 dead and 200 injured (Tota, 2005). The counter-memory of the event initially held the state guilty of being unable to defend its citizens. Two decades with no justice resulted in the counter-memory shifting to one that holds the state accountable for its lack of political and institutional willingness to prosecute the criminals. Extreme views go one step further to accuse the state of carrying out the attack itself. This counter-memory is sustained by civil societies, and memorials play a role in this.

Since the first anniversary, and two decades later, the memorial for the event has been carried out with the same fervour, with the railway station in Bologna being the site of the memorial services. Tota (2005) highlights these as the reasons why this is the case:

> They seem to be contained in a very active and "sane" local civil society with a long tradition of being active in cultural and civic associations, a very efficient local government, a very strong association of victims' relatives with charismatic leaders able to make the voice and the point of view of the victims heard in the city's public discourse, and an art system capable of sustaining, expressing, and providing visibility to the counter-memory of this event.
>
> (Tota, 2005, p 65)

These ingredients, in synergy, constitute the "perfect remembering". This sustains people's hopes and their fight for justice while containing the spirit of the democratic state within it.

In the case of Naples, however, the "imperfect forgetting" is observed. On 23 December 1984, another railway bombing took place in Val di Sambro on the 904 train. This train was moving from Naples to Milan. This bombing occurred during transit at the San Benedetto Val di Sambro tunnel. This site could not be used as it is on the track, and thus the memorial services lost a symbolic space. This, coupled with persistent efforts by the Camorra, the Italian Mafia who are believed to be behind the attacks, to impede all manner of memorial services through violence and lobbying, has led to inaction, silence and humiliation of the victims and their relatives by the local institutions. This state of "imperfect forgetting" is work-intensive, aimed at silencing witnesses and destroying all symbols pertaining to the event.

In Madrid on 11 March 2004, ten explosions took place across four commuter trains travelling from Alcalá de Henares to the southeast of Madrid. In this case, what was interesting was the narrative behind who perpetrated the attack. The elections were around the corner and the government attributed the blame to ETA (Euskadi Ta Askatasuna), a Basque separatist group, despite evidence suggesting Al Qaeda was behind the attacks. After the ruling party lost the election on 14 March 2004, the cover-up came to light with allegations coming from newspaper agencies both national and international. Thus, the 'official' attempts to shape the memory failed while the counter-memory ended up becoming the public memory during the initial years. Presently, the memorialization processes in Madrid are strongly contested, with different groups organizing different memorial events autonomously on 11th March (Toribio Medina, 2024). This was the result of poor institutional handling of the event, its aftermath and the memorialization process. With regard to the globalization of the memorial, Tota (2005) has offered a hypothesis that international forces could influence the memorial. The Madrid explosions signalled the state of terrorism in a globalized world, with memorials being influenced by international forces as well. On the international stage after the Madrid attacks, the European Union declared the European Remembrance Day for Victims of Terror. This day has since been used to commemorate the victimsof terrorism internationally and serves as a stage for the voices of victims and survivors. Recently, Sørensen et al. (2019) have highlighted the influence of international forces on the design of memorials, the process of memorialization and the language used in memorialization. Ibreck (2016) argued that international agendas strongly influenced the construction of memorials in Rwanda to remember the genocide. International donors played a crucial role in the construction of memorials, indicating a departure from memorials being a national act (Ibreck, 2016). Thus, Tota's (2005) hypothesis has come to pass in the globalized world, indicated by the increasing influence of international forces on a nation state's memorial.

The above examples and theories enable us to locate two aspects within a terror event: the "official memory" and the "counter-memory". They also enable us to understand exactly how the memory is being propagated, along with linguistic, semiotic and performative aspects of the memory, as the way to understand how the memory is being constructed. The importance of memory in shaping people's perspectives has been well documented, and this becomes especially true during a terror event. Official memory shapes the response to the event by the government, and seeing if a counter-memory was formed amongst the survivors shows us whether the government response was adequate or insufficient.

Thus, memory becomes the first key aspect that must be analysed and understood if one needs to understand the situation that terror survivors find themselves in during the aftermath of terror attacks.

Social Science Conception of Hope and Hopelessness

Hope allows one to gain agency and voice. Freire (1994) locates hope as an integral part of what makes humans function. Webb (2007) has observed that there is no definitive account of "what it is to hope" and has therefore divided hope into various categories. These categories are not integral to the study at hand; what does matter is that hope be treated as a capacity to look forward to the future.

Hope is affected by the process of sense-making and this process is situated within an imperfect and non-egalitarian society. This results in hope being distributed unevenly as people with greater economic and social resources can hope 'better'.

Hope should not be confused as simply a positive resource. In the current era, hope has often been used in the political game. The United States under the Obama administration has often used hope to justify heavy security measures (Wrangel, 2019). This converts hope into a biotechnology, and its use as a technology creates the "us" and "them" categorization depending on a person's relation to hope (Wrangel, 2019). Hope is also is used to maintain the status quo by those in power. By invoking the idea of hope for a better future, the powers that be maintain the current state of things, even if they are below par for the civilians who live in these conditions. Essentially, hope is offered to those that the world does not want to offer anything else to, as studies have highlighted (Povinelli, 2011; Appadurai, 2013; Lindroth & Sinevaara-Niskanen, 2018). These include the people affected by poverty, climate change or marginalization or maybe all three; i.e. people who have nothing but hope (Lindroth & Sinevaara-Niskanen, 2019). An important aspect to understand is that in the case of the politics of hope, the word 'hope' itself is never used, and instead, "desirable" objects of hope are put up to be served to the people (Lindroth & Sinevaara-Niskanen, 2019). This is possible because people in governance often assume that this is the "hope" that people need and therefore put it out there. Such state-defined connotations of hope have been referred to as "official hope" in the subsequent sections of this study. Essentially, official hope is a tool to maintain inequality and make promises for the future that are often broken. Therefore, the idea of hope is less than useful in a study of terror survivors. Instead, one must explore the idea of hopelessness and the power it holds.

An example of hope's failings is found in Sierra Leone. After the civil war in Sierra Leone, a truth commission was established to enact transitional justice (Ottendörfer, 2019). For the sake of legitimizing its existence, the truth commission instilled in people the hope that things could turn out better through the transitional justice efforts. This hope instillation is possible because the future is uncertain for the most part, and this void of uncertainty can be filled with hope, which mobilized people towards aiding the efforts of the truth commission (Ottendörfer, 2019). This was especially important in Sierra Leone, where the people had always chosen to forget the past rather than engage with it, which is what the truth commission chose to do. The truth commission wanted to begin a process of reconciliation, which was different from what the people wanted. So, on public platforms, people iterated their need for material support.

The demand for material support was present from the beginning, which resulted in the emergence of the "Amputees and War Wounded Association" (AWWA). The AWWA was established with the help of Sierra Leonean Non-Governmental Organisations (NGOs) to demand material support from the truth commission as one of their first actions (Ottendörfer, 2019). The pressure from AWWA eventually caused the truth commission to agree to provide material support after its mandate was accomplished. This is an example of people forcing the commission to align with their hopes rather than the hope defined by the commission.

However, in engaging with the commission, the people were still being disciplined by the actions of the commission. They had to ensure that they followed the process set before them by the commission if they wanted to receive the benefits.

In the end, the commission failed to live up to the hopes that it had set up. They could not fulfil the hopes of the people either. This resulted in reinforcing the people's negative beliefs towards the government. The government had simply failed them once again. Along with this negative belief, the failure of their hopes also increased competition amongst the people, as they believed that some individuals were receiving better benefits than they were. This negatively impacted solidarity.

Thus, the failure of hope is one of the factors that led to disillusionment amongst the people. This understanding is extremely important in conflict and terror scenarios as it is caused by humans and therefore it is up to the state, which is often directly or indirectly the cause (either due to causing the incident or because it failed to prevent it), to rectify the situation.

This disillusionment leads to hopelessness, which is often present amongst terror survivors because of the failure of official channels. Hopelessness may lead to anger and competition, as can be seen in the Sierra Leone example.

Hopelessness is therefore an important aspect to be explored amongst terror survivors.

Through this study, we try to see if a linkage between hopelessness and counter-memory can also be established. While the Bologna example showed us an immediate formation of counter-memory because of anger, we hypothesize that counter-memory can be formed as a result of sustained hopelessness in the state efforts to aid the terror survivors after the event.

Another aspect that needs to be explored is the linkages between official memory and official hope. As both are shaped by official channels and narratives, it becomes important to see how these influence each other.

Social Science Conception of Aspirations

In the discussion about Sierra Leone in the hope section, the idea of people's hopes being let down, leading them to disillusionment, has been discussed. However, it was also stated that this was only one of the factors that led to disillusionment. There is another factor: the dashing of the dreams themselves. The people wanted certain material benefits from the truth commission, and their hope had been that they would receive these. The denial of these materials is what led to their hopelessness. Therefore, there is a need to look at one more factor beyond just hope, which is aspiration. Hope and aspirations are treated differently by Hart (2016) in their study on aspirations. Aspirations are defined as follows:

> Are they akin to hopes, wishes, dreams, ambitions and goals? Do they signal optimism for the future or pessimism about the present? Do they portray longings and yearnings for that which we are not, or cannot do, or do not have? Are aspirations grounded in rationality, emotion, idealism or pragmatism? The answers are not at all straightforward since there are many interpretations and applications of the notion of aspiration. In different contexts it might be argued that aspirations can be all of these things and more. I would argue that aspirations are future-oriented, driven by conscious and unconscious motivations and they are indicative of an individual or group's commitments towards a particular trajectory or end point.
>
> (Hart, 2016, p. 325)

Aspirations encompass tangible and intangible wants and needs and therefore reach out far more widely than hope. Hope is a means to bolster oneself to achieve these aspirations; however, it need not be the only driving force. Through this study, we wish to see if aspirations can be driven by hopelessness and anger rather than hope. This is the missing link in the Sierra Leone study. It is not simply that people had their hopes dashed that led to the disillusionment. There were tangibles involved that the people were hoping towards.

The denial of these tangibles resulted in their hopes being destroyed and led to disillusionment.

There is a need to understand other aspects of aspirations as well. Aspirations do not emerge in isolation from the societal and cultural context but instead emerge through an interaction with that context. Aspirations can be understood to emerge through memories, counter-memories, lived and felt experiences, and social interaction. Aspirations are multi-dimensional, temporal and vary in scale; they can be dormant and emerge over time. They can be shared amongst a group or be individual.

Aspirations are also shaped and constrained by many factors, and people may not be keen to share their entire "aspiration set"; therefore, the revealed aspirations may only form a portion of people's "aspiration sets".

> The choice of aspirations might be influenced to varying degrees by what Bourdieu called the "habitus" of an individual. Habitus is related to the cultural and familial roots from which a person grows. Bourdieu explained that habitus, "operates below the level of calculation and consciousness" and that the, "conditions of existence" influence the formation of habitus which is manifested in the agent's "tastes, practices and works thus constituting a particular lifestyle".
>
> (Bordieu, 2010, p. 166, as cited in Hart, 2016, p.330)

The last important aspect to keep in mind is that aspirations need not emerge from just optimism. Pessimism can also result in aspirations of wanting to break free from their current cycle of life and towards achieving a better life. These aspirations can be seen as counter-aspirations This is where memory, counter-memory, hopelessness and aspirations can intersect in the context of terror. Counter-aspirations may serve as the final link between memory, counter-memory, hope and hopelessness to allow for a greater understanding of the marginalization of terror survivors and differential recovery trajectories. Through this study, we may yet see the establishment of this linkage. It may also allow for plotting a way forward that is divorced from hope and instead fuelled by action around the counter-aspirations expressed by survivors.

Exploring Memory, Hope and Aspirations to Understand Distress and Recovery

In disaster studies, memory, hope and aspirations have often been explored exclusive of each other. The social repair approach to recovery (Aijazi, 2015) argues that memory and hope are important to ensure the recovery of survivors. Moving forward, the study seeks to further illustrate how memory, hope and aspirations and their social situatedness shape survivors' individual distress and their differential recovery trajectories. While memory and hope have been explored in relation to disasters and disaster recovery, aspirations and their impact on recovery have not been explored to the same degree. Hope has been explored as an aspirational capacity that aids in recovery (Appadurai, 2004) but aspirations amount to more than just hope. This has been explored in greater detail within this chapter. Along with exploring aspirations, there is a need to understand how aspirations are inspired by memory and hope. The denial of hope and aspirations is often understood as setting back recovery. While this is true, it does not necessarily end the process of recovery. This study seeks to explore life beyond hope. Some studies, such as, Ottendörfer (2019), have explored the scenario of disillusionment; however, they have not explored it in relation to memory and aspirations.

Memory, on the other hand, has been extensively studied by various disciplines using different worldviews. The psychological and neurobiological understanding of memory is primarily static, linear and located within the physical brain. Whereas memory in the social sciences has been viewed as a collective process. Drawing from the social science literature, this study has demarcated memory into three separate categories: official memory, counter-memory and public memory. Official memory is the memory of an event propagated through state narratives of the event and its aftermath, as well as through state-sponsored memorials for the event. Counter-memory, on the other hand, is the memory constructed by the communities and their associates that is opposed to and contradicts the "official" version of the events (Tota, 2005). The final category used within this study is public memory. Public memory, in this study, is defined as the memory associated with an event as remembered by the general population, i.e., communities and institutions not directly affected by the event and its aftermath. The delineation of these categories is important for understanding the marginalization of survivors in the aftermath of terror events and is dealt with in subsequent sections. Official memory, often considered to be state-driven narratives, may be disconnected from the reality of the event and its aftermath. This dissonance between reality and the official memory can result in the formation of counter-memory, shaped primarily by their lived experiences. The study thus explores the processes that unfold in the formation of counter-memory.

Social science research within trauma and terror studies has been largely focused on collective memory (official, public and counter-memory) and its implications for identity and agency of terror survivors on a collective scale. These studies thus challenge the nature of memory that is engaged within the psychological and neurobiological schools of thought and illustrate its implications for the neglect of the collective nature of distress. While the psychological and neurobiological perspectives engage with the interface between trauma and memory, towards explaining and treating individual-level psychological distress, the social science research focus on individual distress has been limited, resulting in the sidelining of the same in mainstream therapeutic practice and policy. This research study attempts to bridge this gap between individual and collective memory and distress. Moving beyond identity and agency, the most studied social science concepts in relation to terror survivors within trauma, memory and terror studies, the study explores its interlinkages to distress. The close interlinkages of hope/hopelessness and aspirations with the concepts of trauma, memory, identity and agency, and the conceptual fit within the alternative ontological position that situates trauma and memory within the social and cultural context, lead us to hope and aspirations as the means of exploring the co-affective relationship between the survivor and the world they are situated in.

In essence, this study not only explores the relationship between memory, hope and aspiration but it also goes further to explore the emergence of disillusionment, hopelessness, counter-memory and counter-aspirations over the years, differentially shaping individual distress and recovery trajectories among survivors. This can aid in providing a holistic view on terror survivors, their distress and their recovery trajectories, which in turn can aid in developing comprehensive measures to aid these survivors.

Capturing Trajectories of Lived and Felt Experiences

The "lived" experiences of people affected by the event are central to this study. Lived experiences account for memories, hope and aspirations. However, it is not a one-sided relationship. Memories and aspirations influence the lived and felt experiences of the survivors as well, creating a feedback loop. Lived experiences have been used in several studies ranging from psychology to education, including disasters and terror events. Lived experiences capture the world from the lens of the survivors and through their lived experiences; this study situates their memories and aspirations, which in turn inform their actions.

The psychological consequences of surviving a terror attack are vast and varied; a spectrum of distress responses is possible based on exposure and proximity to the event and the survivors of the event. Cultural research that attempts to document the lived experiences of survivors has encountered another arena that implores inquiry. Cultural researchers realize that not all experience is "lived"; instead, the nature of the very experience is diverse and incommensurable, irreducible, often wordless. How does one then document the "felt" experience? How does one embody such materiality of the "body that feels?" Fear, disgust, intensity of dread, horror, anxiety, unease, apprehension and other distress responses that are felt require newer methodological approaches. The "affect" that is felt in the body informs knowledge production through qualitative research strategies with a "focus on immateriality, flux and bodily engagement" (Knudsen & Stage, 2015). The study of such complex and nuanced felt experience, whose articulation is "messy", is necessary as verbal and linguistic expressions are often inadequate. However, it also poses dilemmas of ethics. For instance, how must the cultural researcher probe without triggering a response? The researcher must recognize that a study of affect is a deeply confrontational process for the survivor, and therefore such affective methodologies must reflect on ethical concerns and attempt to resolve the same methodological tensions that it poses (Mehrabi, 2018). Collaborative, narrative processes without strict time demands, envisioned as opening spaces for emotional and emotive articulation that survivors willingly participate in, must be a necessary prerequisite.

Cultural research practice must reinvent itself and bring about methodological innovations to develop nuanced and newer ways of seeing and observing felt experience by paying attention to emotion and affects while simultaneously questioning how cultural processes shape emotion and how emotion in turn shapes the social and cultural (Kahl, 2019).

Affective processes have several critical associations with memory. Often, memories of terror event manifest as post-event distress such as numbness, isolation, disconnection, withdrawal, insomnia, persisting anxiety or fear. French philosopher Jacques Derrida coined the neologism "hauntology" that combines the words "haunting" and "ontology" to depict repetitive and persistent elements of the social and cultural pasts that recur, often to the psychosocial detriment of persons (Derrida, 1994, p. 123). Terror events, one may argue, are no less than such kinds of hauntological experiences. The complex inner worlds of sentient life, i.e., lives that feel deeply through the process of repetitive, haunting and tenacious remembering, require methodologies that privilege deep feeling (Knudsen & Stage, 2015). Affective methodologies recognize that memory is fallible, and therefore a reliance on memory and its verbalization will bring about subjectivities. A distinction between a memory of the feeling and the feeling itself must be drawn, and it takes a skilled researcher to make this discernment. The ontology of memory that conceptualizes both collective memory (official/public/counter-memory) and personal memory as co-constituted utilizes these very subjectivities, highlighted by affective methodologies, to capture the interlinkages between collective and personal memory and its change over time in different contexts. It explores further the so-called subjectivities for a deeper understanding of the social situatedness of trauma memory. It enables the re-conceptualization of trauma memory, known to be fallible/distorted/disrupted/disjointed/repetitive/intrusive, as co-constituted, dynamic and temporally emerging in a non-linear fashion. The study documents and makes available not just the narratives but also the feelings associated with the memories being shared, by creating space for the survivors' narratives to be told in their own voices. The use of a relational approach over an extended period, as detailed in the methodology section, too enabled the study to do justice to the exploration of felt experiences. Further, the study utilized the medium of creative representation to portray the multi-layered lived reality of the survivors. However, owing to the limitations of representation in the given form, the book falls short of capturing the creative representations emerging from the AAPTI project. A glimpse of the same is available as the 26/11 Memories, Hope and Way Forward: Virtual Exhibition (https://youtu.be/SBrH4F_KoeQ). Above all, the study's engagement with time, beyond being just a contextual factor, enabled it to illustrate the lived and felt experiences as they unfolded over time.

Approach and Methodology

As the study is concerned with the marginalization of civilian survivors in the aftermath of the terror attack, the pragmatic world view was found to be the best fit. It pushes for practical solutions from within existing available resources to address the issue and not rely on grand narratives and the politics of overhaul (Stroud, 2023). To be able to arrive at pragmatic real-life solutions that could work, one cannot be restricted to any particular disciplinary understanding and strategies but must be able to transcend disciplinary boundaries and choose research strategies, methods and data sources that adequately address the problem in hand. Thus, drawing from the pragmatic world view, the study uses mixed methodology to comprehensively understand the marginalization of civilian survivors in the aftermath of terror attacks and explores the way forward in addressing the same. The pragmatic world view and the mixed methodology also align with the alternative ontology and epistemological positions taken up for the study, which necessitate the bringing together of data from several sources on trauma and memory from the subjective and intersubjective realms.

The methods detailed here were used to capture both the macro-structural processes and the lived and felt experiences of survivors. The macro-structural processes, shaping memory post the terror events, including memorialization, illustrate official and public memories, hopes and aspirations. The lived and felt experiences captured through survivors' narratives illustrate memory, hopes, aspirations, hopelessness, counter-memory and counter-aspirations, from the individual survivor's perspective over the years. Thus, the methodology allows for a comprehensive engagement with the concept of memory both at the collective/macro-structural and personal/micro-individual level and explores their interfaces in shaping differential trajectories of recovery and distress. Going beyond the illustration of macro-social and cultural structures that play out in the aftermath of a terror event, the study attempts to illustrate its manifestations in the survivors' everyday lives by capturing their lived and felt experiences using survivor narratives. The felt and lived experiences of the survivors open up the possibility of arriving at grounded pragmatic solutions to the marginalization of terror survivors.

The method for capturing the macro-structural processes shaping memory, including memorialization, was as follows: To understand the memory of trauma at a collective/structural level, the study explored media coverage of memorials and other secondary data sources such as newspapers, web and journal articles, national and international policy documents, acts, schemes and programmes related to the 26/11 terror attack. The exploration of the media coverage of the memorials was intended to capture data on various memorials for 26/11 and other terror events in the past, reported in the public domain (print and online media). The study used Google Reverse Image Search on Google Images along with certain key words to find the source of the image and the related news item. The time frame for the memorial collation was from 2009 (i.e., a year after the 26/11 attacks, and in this backdrop 2008 has been left out) to 2019.

To augment the accuracy of the results of the Google Reverse Image Search, a defined set of keywords was used including: *26/11 terror attack, Tribute, Homage, Mumbai, Candles, Victims, Remembering, Strength, Stories, The Taj, Chabad, Nariman House* and *CST*. These key words enabled precise tracking of the image sources and associated news clippings. Key words play a vital role in filtering image searches as they help to locate the original publication sources and retrieve visuals that are specific, such as tributes, memorial events, citizens' gatherings and other acts of public remembering associated with the 26/11 attacks.

Reverse image search helps to quickly discover visually similar images from around the web. The process involves using the snipping tool (on Windows) to cut an image from anywhere and then uploading that image on Google Reverse Image Search. Another website similar to 'reverse image search' is "prepostseo.com", wherein images can be uploaded to find similar photos on the web. Every image or news clipping of memorial events was documented in Excel to create a database. The final database had 144 entries of memorial events after removing duplicate reporting of the same event. Some of these news clippings identified were accompanied by images, while others were standalone text-based reports. While standalone images were categorized visually, clippings were assessed for both content and visual elements. For instance, standalone images were categorized based on subjects in the image, markers of identification such as uniformed personnel or an image of commemoration. Therefore, uniforms or official memorial sites indicated personnel, while public figures were recognized through media presence or official roles. Civilians were identified as members of the public, often depicted in candlelight vigils or group tributes.

The images and the news items were further analysed to categorize the memorials based on their focus on civilians, personnel and public figures. The place of the memorial/tribute was also taken into consideration in the classification process. "Civilians" include what we call "commoners" or common persons. The personnel category includes police and armed forces, along with any instance where "martyr" is mentioned, and/or the event took place at the Police Memorial Site (Mumbai Gymkhana), which is also included in this category unless it is a public figure paying tribute. Thirdly, the public figure category comprises Chief Ministers, Prime Ministers, Presidents, celebrities and even those who gained a certain prominence after the 26/11 attack. Some individuals, like the Director of the Chabad Relief Fund, Anant Goenka (Executive Director, Indian Express), the then Rabbi of Chabad including the then-baby Moshe, and the Air India building where a laser tribute was held, have been classified as 'Public Figures'.

In making this classification, "Public Figures" are considered to be those who are known to the public and have a certain social position and/or significant influence over the public. The Memorial collation includes only headlines and images from news dailies and weekly's and thus excludes any private tributes and personal social media posts. In making the collation, a distinction has been made between online media memorial coverage and all other tributes that poured in for 26/11, which were excluded from the analysis.

To further account for the official memories, hope and aspirations, the study analysed the following secondary sources of data to triangulate the findings emerging from the analysis of memorials.

Official memory, hope and aspirations were captured using the narratives and depictions of the event in the public arena beyond memorialization. This was done through a systematic review of newspapers, web and journal articles. This process presented a wide range of narratives circulated at the time, allowing for a thorough elucidation of the various views and agendas presented on the event and how it was/is chosen to be remembered.

A combination of visual and textual analysis was employed to examine the nature of public remembering and memorialization of the 26/11 attacks. Images and textual references to the memorialization were traced through defined keywords and thematically grouped to augment the specificity of search results. A dataset of images was compiled for the period between 2009 and 2019 (ten anniversaries of 26/11 attacks) to identify whether media subjects were civilians, personnel or public figures. This compilation of anniversaries each year facilitates a longitudinal comprehension of public memorialization. Based on these views and agendas, an examination of "hope" as presented in the public arena was distilled as "official hope" based on the concept of "hope as a biotechnology" (Wrangel, 2019).

Finally, the official aspirations born out of these memories and hopes were identified. One set of aspirations focused on heightened securitization in the aftermath of the event. The next set was the rights of and compensation for the survivors. This was done through an examination of policy documents at the international level, followed by an examination of Acts, schemes and policy documents at the national level. This was done to understand the rights and compensations for terror survivors on a global scale. The Acts and schemes at the national level were examined alongside the context to understand their implications for the terror survivors.

The methodology utilized to capture the lived and felt experiences of individual survivors primarily relied on survivor narratives gathered in

2017–2018, towards understanding the recovery trajectories of survivors over 10 years and the narratives from the process documentation of the AAPTI project from 2008 to 2014. The primary study in 2017–2018 selected 30 people each from the 26/11 and 13/7 terror attacks, using cluster sampling (K-means clusters formed based on the extent of support received by the survivors of the AAPTI project, to ensure the inclusion of both the least and maximally served survivors). However, in this study, largely narratives of 30, 26/11 survivors have been analysed, along with a few narratives of 13 July 2011 triple blast survivors, as they provide a unique vantage point of access to survivor narratives immediately after the event. The study uses the narrative analysis approach as it captures the survivors' perspectives, by focusing on how the narratives are structured, along with the context in which they are narrated, and how meanings are differently shaped. The compilation of the narratives over 10 years from the process documentation of the AAPTI project enabled engagement with time beyond being just a contextual factor. The changing narratives, their context and meanings could be captured from the narratives of survivors documented from the first day of contact with the AAPTI case managers (immediately after the event) to that of the tenth-year research, which captured the narratives of recovery trajectories. The process documentation comprises reports of initial visits at the hospital; initial and subsequent follow-up home visits; rapid needs assessment; detailed psychosocial needs assessment; health camps; mental health assessments; support service request-related assessments; visits to the project office etc., by volunteers, interns, counsellors and case managers. The interns who worked during the initial phase of the AAPTI project joined as case managers, thus allowing for an uninterrupted relationship over 5 years (2009–2014), and for a deeper understanding of the lived and felt experiences of the survivors, the changing context both personal and collective, and the different trajectories of recovery unfolding with time. One of the case managers conducted the data collection for the tenth-year research study on recovery trajectories as a researcher independent of the project programme team and the funders, to elicit the most candid narratives that focused on the key highlights of the past ten years, the imagination of life without the terror event, how the event affected their everyday lives, reflections on interventions and their usefulness, gaps in support services and the way forward. This also enabled the study to capture both the continuity and discontinuities in the narrative over the years and to dwell deeper into the same in relation to the changing personal and collective context.

The closest research designs that would match the above description would be the Life Course Research method, a method that captures individuals' lives over extended periods of time. This method evolves with the phenomenon over time and (in its various applications) not only allows for a deeper understanding of the everyday lived and felt experiences of the survivors but also captures the interface between the macro-structural (intersubjective) and micro-individual (subjective) level dimensions of trauma and memory. The methodology used in this study combines the various possibilities that the life course research method offers to explore social structure, intersectionality, individual choices/agency, and identity within the changing social, political, cultural and personal contexts, in comprehensively understanding the interface of trauma and memory in shaping differential recovery trajectories. The life course research method also aligns with the ontological and epistemological positions of the study as it allows for: the focus on change over time, allowing the study to capture the dynamic nature of the phenomenon; the emphasis on the interface between the individual and the context (contextual understanding); the exploration of how the survivors' lived and felt experiences dynamically change with the changes in personal, social, political, cultural or historical contexts that they are situated in; and a holistic perspective not only with regard to changes over time but with regard to the understanding of the phenomenon at the intersections of both the collective and personal levels. In line with the ontological and epistemological position of the study and the critiques of life course research, it takes caution in not: treating lived experiences, trauma and memory as a series of distinct stages, events or processes, that follow a linear trajectory; and getting carried away by social determinism or individualism, but explores the interface between the collective and the personal in a comprehensive manner.

References

Aijazi, O. (2015). Theorizing a social repair orientation to disaster recovery: Developing insights for disaster recovery policy and programming. *Global Social Welfare*, *2*(1), 15–28.

Appadurai, A. (2004). The capacity to aspire: Culture and the terms of recognition. In V. Rao & M. Walton (Eds.), *Culture and public action* (pp. 59–94). Stanford: Stanford University Press.

Appadurai, A. (2013). *The future as cultural fact. Essays on the global condition*. Verso.

Assmann, J. (1992). *Das kulturelle Gedächtnis: Schrift, Erinnerung und politische Identität in frühen Hochkulturen* [Cultural memory: Writing, remembering, and political identity in ancient cultures]. Beck

Beall, J. (2007). Cities, terrorism and urban wars of the 21st century.

Bourdieu, P. (2010). Distinction. London: Routledge.

Bracken, P. (2002). *Trauma: Culture, meaning and philosophy*. Whurr Publishers.

Brockmeier, J. (2002). Remembering and forgetting: Narrative as cultural memory. *Culture & Psychology*, *8*(1), 15–43.

Crenshaw, M. (1981). The causes of terrorism. *Comparative politics*, *13*(4), 379-399.

Derrida, J. (1994). *Specters of Marx, the state of the debt, the work of mourning, & the new international* (P. Kamuf, Trans.). Routledge. ISBN 9780415389570.

Freire, P. (1994). *Pedagogy of hope: Reliving pedagogy of the oppressed*. Continuum.

Gross, D. (2000). *Lost time: On remembering and forgetting in late modern culture*. University of Massachusetts Press.

Hart, C. S. (2016). How do aspirations matter?. *Journal of Human Development and Capabilities*, *17*(3), 324–341.

Ibreck, R. (2016). International constructions of national memories: The aims and effects of foreign donors' support for genocide remembrance in Rwanda. In Jenkins, T. (Ed.), *Political culture, soft interventions and nation building* (pp. 31–51). Routledge.

Kahl, A. (2019). *Analyzing affective societies: Methods & methodologies*. Routledge.

Knudsen, B. T., & Stage, C. (2015). Introduction: Affective methodologies. In Stage, E. B. (Ed.), *Affective methodologies: Developing cultural research strategies for the study of affect* (p. 2). Palgrave Macmillan, UK.

Lindroth, M., & Sinevaara-Niskanen, H. (2018). *Global politics and its violent care for indigeneity: Sequels to colonialism*. Palgrave Macmillan.

Lindroth, M., & Sinevaara-Niskanen, H. (2019). Politics of hope. *Globalizations*, *16*(5), 644–648.

Mehrabi, T. (2018). Being intimate with flies: On affective methodologies and laboratory work. *Køn & Forskning*, *1*, 73–80.

Ottendörfer, E. (2019). Assessing the role of hope in processes of transitional justice: Mobilizing and disciplining victims in Sierra Leone's truth commission and reparations programme. *Globalizations*, *16*(5), 649–663.

Povinelli, E. A. (2011). *Economies of abandonment: Social belonging and endurance in late liberalism* (Vol. 48). Duke University Press.

Rasmussen, S. (2002). The uses of memory. *Culture & Psychology*, *8*(1), 113–129.

Sørensen, M. L. S., Viejo-Rose, D., & Filippucci, P. (2019). Memorials and memorialisation: History, forms, and affects. In: Sørensen, M., Viejo-Rose, D., Filippucci, P. (Eds.), *Memorials in the Aftermath of Armed Conflict* (pp. 1–32). Palgrave Studies in Cultural Heritage and Conflict. Palgrave Macmillan, Cham..

Stroud, S. R. (2023). *The evolution of pragmatism in India: An intellectual biography of BR Ambedkar*. Harper Collins.

Terdiman, R. (1993). *Present past: Modernity and the memory crisis*. Cornell University Press.

Toribio Medina, M. (2024). 20 years on. A walk through the memorialisation of the 11M attacks. In: Karcher, K., Dimcheva, Y., Toribio Medina, M., Parkes, M. (Eds.), *Urban terrorism in contemporary Europe: Remembering, imagining and anticipating violence* (pp. 47–67). Springer International Publishing.

Tota, A. L. (2005). Terrorism and collective memories: Comparing bologna, naples and madrid 11 March. *International Journal of Comparative Sociology*, *46*(1–2), 55–78.

Webb, D. (2007). Modes of hoping. *History of the Human Sciences*, *20*(3), 65–83.

Wrangel, C. T. (2019). Biopolitics of hope and security: Governing the future through US counterterrorism communications. *Globalizations*, *16*(5), 664–677.

3 In Memoriam: Remembering and Hoping in Space

The 26/11 attacks on Mumbai, although devastating, have been etched in public memory to showcase human efforts as survivors rebuild their lives in the face of grave adversity. Governmental efforts have brought together affected groups to reconstruct the city and reinforce commitment to public safety. Monuments, memorials, annual commemorations, gatherings and ceremonies bring about collectivization of people and serve as a unifying force to perform acts of remembrance. These events create spaces for mourning, reflection, solidarity and paying homage to the martyrs. Political discourse and media depictions shape public memory and keep the event alive in societal consciousness.

Remembering 26/11

The events of 26/11 had a profound impact on the Indian psyche and the global community. The vulnerability of cities to targeted terror attacks brought with it a wave of panic about intelligence failures and a need for coordinated intelligence efforts across and between nations presented itself. The terror attacks drew widespread condemnation as over 165 persons were killed and 300 wounded. The predominant cause of mortality was victims sustaining bullet injuries to vital organs and delayed evacuation times (Bhandarwar & Tayade, 2012).

On the night of 26th November 2008, ten-armed terrorists struck simultaneously at five different locations in Mumbai. These locations were the luxury hotels Oberoi-Trident and the Taj Palace and Tower, the Leopold Café, the Chabad House Jewish Cultural Centre and the Chhatrapati Shivaji Terminus, simply known as CST or VT (Victoria Terminus) in popular parlance. The attack did, however, diverge beyond these locations. Two taxis with explosives detonated at Vile Parle, a western Mumbai suburb and Dockyard Road, close to the Mazagaon Dock that is famous for manufacturing warships and submarines for the Indian Navy. Two of the terrorists who had opened fire at CST travelled to Cama Hospital, where a shootout took place. The attackers were finally brought down at Girgaum Chowpatty. At this location, one of

DOI: 10.4324/9781003684954-3

the terrorists was killed while the other, Mohammed Ajmal Kasab, was the only terrorist to be captured alive, owing to the heroic act and martyrdom of Tukaram Omble, assistant sub-inspector of the Mumbai police.

The casualties vary across news articles and official documents, but approximately 140 Indians and 25 foreign nationals were killed in the attack; more than 300 people were injured. The attack turned into a three-day siege that ended after the Mumbai Police and security forces captured one terrorist alive and killed nine. Figure 3.1 depicts the portrayal of the event as reflected in media depictions.

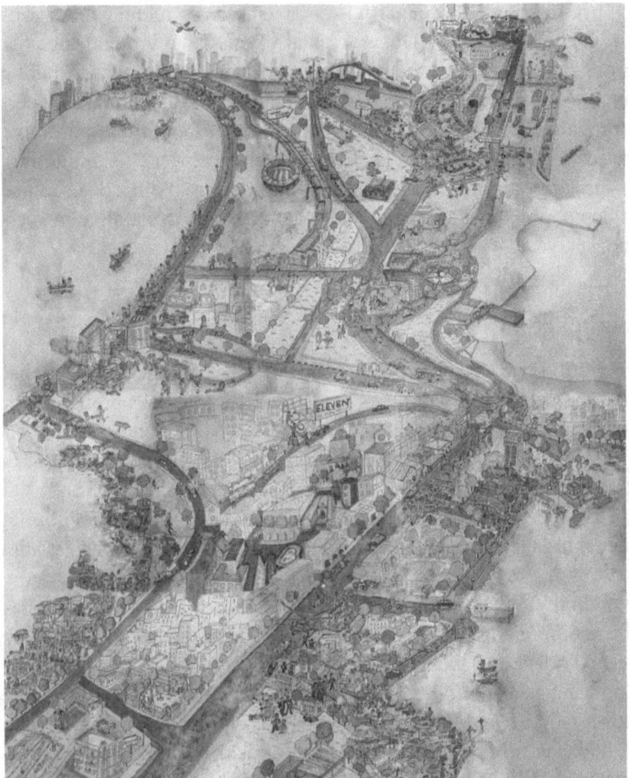

Figure 3.1 Hand-drawn map of Mumbai depicting the flow of events during 26/11

Source: Creative Credits – Ms Pritha Choudhury (Artist), Research Officer, TISS and Mr Kartikey Karnatak (Designer), Media Consultant, TISS

The devastating effects of the attack continue to ripple across time to this day. However, along with the pain and many expressions of anguish came solidarity. In the wake of the attack, tributes came pouring in expressing support to those who were affected, and these tributes and memorials continue to pop up every year on the anniversary of the event. However, one needs to ask a pertinent question: who are the people prominently remembered in these tributes? Why and what implications does it carry? In creating such memorials, governments of the day speak of resilience and unity and portray events such as 26/11 as a story of strength and the indomitable spirit of the people. Public art, literature and other collective embodiments of memorialization reflect this rhetoric of strength, resilience and hope.

The section that follows makes a critical inquiry about the discourse surrounding the official memory of the event and the actions that surrounded the aftermath of the event. This line of inquiry is important because it attempts to unpack what informs the official memory of the event. Commemorations, memorials, monuments and other annual events signifying public and cultural memory foster collective remembrance, highlighting stories of heroism and unity. This shared memory transforms pain into a powerful symbol of enduring strength and future optimism.

Public Memory and Public Hope

The terminology public memory refers to ways in which eventsof historical significance and national importance are remembered and recollected in public discourse. How are official rituals performed? How are the affected people commemorated? Such acts of national remembering that are performed through various institutional mechanisms, such as police tributes and bureaucratic exaltations, become official history. This version is then systematically produced, and they turn into significant chapters in the annals of a nation's history. It infuses a national conspicuousness in ordinary, everyday citizens and helps consolidate a sense of belonging as a member of a national community of wronged citizens. The history-official memory dichotomy preserves the past through the production of an imagery of a wronged nation to such an extent that this is the only persisting image. The everyday struggle of survivors is forgotten, invisiblized or relegated to the margins, only to be called upon to perform an outrage over the wronged nation. The question of survivor rights and justice is peripheral (Ahmed, 2014) yet the "survivor" is sought out every year to become a voice for hope and justice.

The Fourth Estate or the 4th pillar of democracy plays a crucial role in the way public memory and hope are shaped in the aftermath of a terror attack. Survivors' stories are packaged as stories of resilience by the media. The media serves as a platform for individuals to share their experiences, express their grief and seek solidarity with others. The media humanizes the tales of the victims, their families and the first responders by conducting interviews, writing opinion articles and providing live coverage. This encourages empathy among the public. Amid catastrophe, this emotional bond is essential for bringing people together and reaffirming a sense of community.

However, the media often goes beyond commemorations and community building. It raises questions of geopolitical interests, threats to national sovereignty and fosters nationalistic fervour, magnifying external threats and internal preoccupations. This kind of functioning can lead to a very skewed public perception about complex geopolitical realities, increased xenophobia and often results in a call for further militarism.

Every year on the anniversary of 26/11, leading newspapers publish opinion editorials, while news channels host discussions and debates on various issues, including why India opted for a diplomatic approach with Pakistan after the attacks instead of declaring war. With the advent of social media, short jingoistic videos provoke questions on nationalism; these digital narratives too shape and reshape public opinion repeatedly.

In the paper "Journalism Caught in Narrow Nationalism: The India-Pakistan Media War", Bose (2011) argues that the media and journalism are caught in forms of narrow nationalism which he dubs "rival nationalism" Rather than being a watchdog of democracy when reporting terror events, the media takes a partisan approach to issues of geopolitical tensions between warring nations such as India and Pakistan.

The 26/11 terror attacks soured relations between India and Pakistan; prior to this incident, the Kargil War of 1999 had brought geopolitical tensions to the forefront. Max Hastings, a British journalist and military historian, states that, "When the nation is at war, reporting becomes an extension of that war" (Rai, 2000, p. 6). Thus, in such cases, nationalism defeats responsible journalism. Various newspapers called the 26/11 attacks "A war on India" or a "War against Mumbai". The word "war" was used repeatedly by the media, although the Indian government of the day did not declare war against Pakistan (Bose, 2011).

With both nations being nuclear-owning states, the media kept reminding the public at large that the threat of nuclear warfare was perhaps even a possibility. In his work titled *Journalism Caught in Narrow Nationalism: The India-Pak Media War,* Bose (2011, p. 28) writes,

> Pakistan sees India as an arrogant Hindu nation where minority Muslims are made to suffer. India sees Pakistan through the tunnel-vision of Muslim fundamentalism nursing Islamic terrorism. Unfortunately, journalists on both sides wear the same glasses too.

Media coverage of terrorist attacks frequently reflects the intricate interactions between media, politics and society. The lens used by media houses often influences public perception. When the media report these attacks using high-decibel language peppered with nationalistic fervour, these have an impact on international relations and societal dynamics.

In the wake of terrorist acts, jingoism, which is characterized by intense patriotism and is frequently coupled with an aggressive foreign policy, tends to arise as a reaction to perceived threats to national identity and security. Newspapers are important for influencing public opinion since they serve as informational platforms. Media outlets may turn to sensationalizing news in their quest for high readership and profits, reinforcing jingoistic feelings in the process. The narrative often calls for a forceful and coordinated national reaction.

Often media reporting places an inordinate premium on the ethnicity and nationality of the attackers to fuel nationalistic feelings, in turn contributing to the production and perpetuation of negative stereotypes about certain communities.

Repeated coverage of visuals such as candlelight vigils, distraught citizens and flags flying at half-mast fosters a sense of community. Yet such evocative imagery can manufacture an "us versus them" mentality that demonizes not only the attackers but the community the attackers belong to. When the media focuses on the attackers' background in a bid to make jingoistic spectacles out of it, it overgeneralizes the narrative without getting into the nuance and complexity of historical geopolitical factors that influence terrorism.

Although the fourth estate is a significant tool for advocacy and a watchdog of democratic performance, when the machinery gets entrapped in the snares of sensationalism it serves to create division rather than unity and empathy. Nationalism that can serve as a unifying force turns into a divisive force with heightened inter-communal tensions and then polarizes the society.

On the other hand, public hope is the shared optimism and aspiration held by a community or the larger public. It can be informed by several aspects of public life ranging from socio-cultural developments to socio-economic conditions. Religious and spiritual responses to the 26/11 attack range from public gatherings and condemnation of the event, followed by a message for unity and peace. For the 10-year anniversary of the attack in 2018, the *Indian Express*, in collaboration with Facebook, unveiled the "26/11 Stories of Strength", which brought together politicians and artists alike. Movie star Amitabh Bachchan stated, "there is inherent unity to mankind, and we succeed by sharing with others. If a nation is not united, it is not a nation" (Barnagarwala, 2018, Retrieved 2023). Such acts provide a driving force for increased civic engagement and encourage social cohesion through artistic expression.

The setting of terror acts in large cities involves complex interplays between memory, location and trauma. Attack sites become sacred spaces that ingrain communal pain into the urban environment. Converted into memorials, these areas function as hubs for shared mourning and remembrance. These tangible marks form public memory, which is then strengthened by stories of resilience and commemoration occasions. Such places frequently have names of the victims, symbolic architecture and quiet spaces for introspection as part of their architecture of remembrance. These locations are marked by trauma that transforms into a shared narrative of healing and solidarity, preserving the past while inspiring hope for the future.

Memory, Space and Trauma

In recent decades, the discipline of Humanities has expanded its disciplinary orientations to include memory, history, space and trauma within its vast scope. In the post-Holocaust world, the borders and boundaries of various disciplines within the humanities have become porous. Consider this: is it possible to locate and study the horrors of the Holocaust within a singular disciplinary site? As researchers around the world grapple with the multidimensional aspects of inquiry – from psychological, sociological, historical, geopolitical, literary inquiries etc. – several sub-disciplines emerged, given the immense vastness of the Holocaust. Memory Studies, Trauma Studies, Testimony Studies, Holocaust Studies, Jewish Studies and many more emerged as the disciplinary offshoots of this historical horror. Memory is intrinsic and critical to such forms of inquiry spanning visual and performing arts, media studies, urban studies, urban design and architecture.

What links these several forms of disciplinary inquiries are: a) a remembrance of trauma and b) a remembrance of place: where all the horrors occur?

Another significant facet of this culture of memory is the way questions of human rights, justice and the spirit of humanism, whether in the upliftment of the human condition or in the upholding of human dignity, have been embedded into these visual cultures. Various memorials and museums are visual condemnations of apartheid, dictatorships, wars, totalitarianism and segregation (Adorno, 1986). The Robben Island maximum security prison, which housed Nelson Mandela, touts itself as "the unique symbol of the triumph of the human spirit over adversity, suffering and injustice" (Robben Island Museum, Retrieved 2023). Art and architecture serve as vehicles to carry messages of pacifism and justice; the artwork by itself becomes a tool of human meaning-making that directs attention to larger issues.

These memorials are rooted in space and strive to remind future generations of the trauma experienced by individuals and certain communities. Trauma is typically an individual experience when a person experiences a threat to life, bodily integrity, or sanity. Trauma overwhelms the individual's ability to cope and leaves the person in a state of fear of death, torture and emotional distress (Pearlman & Saakvitne, 1995, p. 60). Repeated or repetitive remembering keeps people trapped in trauma and excessive emotional pain.

Such forms of remembering locate incidents in space. In this spatialization of memory, space is remembered vividly, as one cannot separate the event from where it took place. This interconnectedness between space and memory has further made demands on the humanities to create sub-disciplines such as Museum Studies, Memorial Studies, Traumatic Heritage Studies and so on. Space "..conveys meaning, tells stories, constructs values and is a powerful system through which any given society represents itself.." (Violi, 2017, p. 188).

Museums and memorials are thus spaces where memory "resides", and they help convey meanings; these sites preserve those meanings for posterity through the creation of visual narratives. In conventional museums, the primary intent is to create a record of history, a transmission of knowledge about the past, a visual presentation that becomes the primary consumption of the onlooker. Objects in the museum are arranged to inform and notify visitors of a past way of life of specific communities, clans, kingdoms and so on. However, in trauma sites, the intention is not knowledge transmission but a somatization of a tragic past in shaping collective memory and meaning-making through symbolic narratives; such acts of meaning-making are to appeal to the next generations to not repeat history, not to commit crimes against humanity and to not reproduce travesties of justice. Former concentration camps and prisons thus become such sites that preserve memory of the trauma. The visitor to these sites is also transformed; from casual onlookers, they become emotional and affective beings, experiencing a sentience by peeking into the injuries of history. In such sites of trauma, objects are not merely carriers of information and knowledge, but a reminder of a tragedy.

Baby Moshe (Moshe Holtzberg), a survivor of the 26/11 Mumbai attacks, was two years old when his parents, who ran the Chabad House, were killed by terrorists and he was rescued by his nanny, Sandra Samuel. The current Rabbi of the Chabad House has preserved Baby Moshe's room in the same condition as it was during the 26/11 attacks, as a tribute to his parents and a symbol of resilience.

In Baby Moshe's room, his crib and the Hebrew writings by his mother on the walls of his room are prompts for the onlooker to remember the daily sociality of an ordinary family who lived in oblivion until the events of 26/11. The semiotic transformation of a space that once experienced calamity and horror and witnessed a terrible crime against humanity into a memorial alters the way a place is remembered. "Before" and "After" are identifiers to demarcate spatial memory as pre- and post-events. The incident and the memorial project the Mumbai Chabad House onto the world stage and renew discussions around antisemitism and the Holocaust.

Trauma, injury and public remembering may be easily co-opted for political use. Nationalistic history utilizes these sites of remembering to target certain identities of communities, nations and states on the world stage. There is a theatrical quality to these memorials. While the public at large may mourn and grieve, the political class performs jingoism for electoral gains in the backdrop of these memorials.

These memorials are a spatial preservation of the collective stress and trauma faced by human societies from time to time. The built environment of these sites of memory is distinct; space and trauma are implanted into a built structure through a phenomenological mode of operation. In other words, the experience of those hurt, harmed or injured in events of history is preserved in space for others to vicariously experience the same horrors. The materiality of the bodily experience of an injured person from the past is recreated through art, architecture and other tools of history for the next generation. The German philosopher George Hegel famously stated[1] that we learn from history that we do not learn from history. The rising number of memorials is a testament to the rising crimes against humanity around the world.

Memory, Memorial and Monument

Over the years, usually around the anniversary of the 26/11 event, the city's various memorials gain prominence by turning into sites of tribute and commemoration to those who lost their lives. These configurations offer the public an overriding imagery of martyrdom. In turn, recurrent, annual public spectatorship and homage create a fleeting iconography of the event, only for it to resurface at the next anniversary. Between anniversaries, these memorials remain an ordinary feature of the city's public space that a passer-by may perhaps view in a transitory moment of travel. However, the 26/11 anniversary catapults these memorials to sites of affective intensity, a space where remembrance, patriotism and homage to fellow citizens are performed. These memorials are syntaxes of a cultural grammar and produce meaning for intentional visitors every year.

This 'culture of anniversaries' (Brockmeier, 2002) produces deep associations between date, place and event. Memorials are intrinsic to the production of such visual cultures for tributes and grieving; they provide a visually stimulated, sensory methodology to express anguish, engage in panegyric, offer a eulogy and create a space for collective expressions of hope. Spatially, memorials provide opportunities for habitual remembrances and the production of 'the message', usually one of solidarity and triumph of the human spirit against hate and terror.

The first anniversary of the 26/11 attack was commemorated across the city through various public demonstrations of solidarity. Yet, the congregation of people waving the tricolour outside the Taj Mahal Hotel brought attention to the nationalistic urges of public discourse surrounding the terror attack. The Taj was no longer a luxury hotel but a monument serving a "cultural function" (Stubblefield, 2015) instrumental in connecting public memory to history. However, such visuals have enabled the political class to capitalize on this calamity. The first anniversary of the attack evoked furious media coverage and opportunities for jingoism for the groups engaged in various forms of polity (Teltumbde, 2009). Though the tributes are annual affairs in public memory, and the terror event has often been co-opted by narrow nationalistic politics, memorials still mushroom at every anniversary of the event.

Every year, the places that were attacked by the terrorists – from the Chhatrapati Shivaji Terminus, the Leopold Café, Cama Hospital, to the Nariman Chabad House, the Taj Palace and the Oberoi-Trident Hotels – all transform into sites of tribute. Each year, civilians gather on Mumbai's beaches and parks and mourn and remember the martyrs of the attack. Sand artists such as Sudarshan Patnaik create memorable sand sculptures grieving the martyrs and putting forth a message of unity against terrorism.

The *Prerana Sthal*, a bust made in honour of Tukaram Omble, stands tall at the entrance of Chowpatty. Sub-Inspector Omble was instrumental in the capture of Ajmal Kasab, the only terrorist to be caught alive. Omble held on to the barrel of Kasab's rifle as Kasab fired bullets into his chest. This act of Omble's is widely regarded as an ultimate act of duty-fuelled bravery, as this enabled Omble's colleagues to overpower the terrorist. Tukaram Omble's *sthal*, a *chowk* named in honour of Ashok Kamte, the then Additional Commissioner of Police, parks dedicated to Hemant Karkare, Chief of the Anti-Terrorism Squad, Vijay Salaskar of the Mumbai Police and Major Sandeep Unnikrishnan and Gajender Singh of the NSG are memorial tributes that have immortalized the names and martyrdom of the uniformed personnel. Such public parks honouring the slain men are scattered across the city, in Goregaon, Andheri East, Borivali, Jogeshwari-Vikhroli Link Road.

At the city's iconic Marine Drive, outside the Policy Gymkhana, a large Police Memorial stands tall. Touted as one of the largest 26/11 memorials in the city, the memorial comprises a granite plaque that is 26 feet high and 11 feet wide to symbolize the date of the attack. The plaque lists the names of the 18 security personnel who lost their lives protecting the city. They belonged to the Railway Protection Force (RPF), Mumbai Police, Government Railway Police (GRP) and the commandos of the National Security Guards (NSGs). Owing to the construction of the coastal road, the memorial has now been shifted within the compound at the Police Commissionerate at Mumbai Police's headquarters, Crawford Market.

The Taj Mahal Hotel, which became the spatial symbol of the attack, also erected a memorial plaque in the resplendent redesigned lobby area. The plaque commemorates the guests, the hotel staff and security personnel who lost their lives in the grand old hotel. Candlelight vigils are organized every year to remember the people who lived and perished during those tumultuous days.

A grand, granite plaque stands at the passenger concourse for outstation trains at the Chhatrapati Shivaji Terminus. It honours the passengers, railway workers and security staff who died during the attack. The plaque proclaims proudly, "Thc fight against terrorism will continue".

Another granite plaque at the Cama and Albless hospital honours two guards who died in the attack. At the iconic Café Leopold, which is frequented by filmmakers, artists, authors, musicians and the public alike, the bullets from the indiscriminate firing on that fateful night have been preserved.

Box 3.1: Chabad House: A Memorial for Everyone

In the late hours of 26th November 2008, two gunmen stormed the Nariman Lighthouse or the Chabad House, a Jewish religious and cultural centre that provides a space for Jewish travellers in the city. Chabad Houses are situated around the world to impart religious knowledge on Judaism and to provide Judaica services to Jewish travellers. Such services include providing kosher meals to Jews visiting the city, organizing religious seminars, organizing Jewish study classes, amongst other activities of a similar nature. Each Chabad House is run by a Rabbi and a Rebbetzin (title given to the wife of a Rabbi).

The Chabad House located on Hormusji Street in Colaba, Mumbai is one such centre for the Jewish community and visiting Jews in Mumbai. At the time of the 26/11 attack, the Chabad House was run by Rabbi Gavriel Holtzberg and Rebbetzin Rivka Holtzberg.

When the building was targeted by the terrorists, the Rabbi and his wife were brutally murdered while the gunmen held the guests at Chabad House hostage for a while before murdering them. Two floors down, baby Moshe, the child of the Rabbi, was fast asleep in his crib. In a display of exceptional courage and fortitude, Moshe was rescued by his nanny, Sandra Samuel. As the events of 26/11 played out, there was live media coverage telecast around the globe. International, national and local media, along with huge crowds and curious members of the public, gathered outside the Chabad House as NSG commandos combated the terrorists inside the fated site.

A memorial to the victims was inaugurated at Nariman House ten years after the Mumbai attacks. The current Rabbi Israel has turned the Chabad House into a museum and a memorial. Baby Moshe's room has been preserved in the same way it was found the morning after the gunmen were overpowered and killed by security forces. In Moshe's room, one can see several holes in the walls, the place pierced by the terrorists' bullets, Hebrew alphabets handwritten by the Rebbetzin Rivika around the room, the crib where baby Moshe slept, horizontal pencil markings denoting Moshe's height every few months and small reminders that tell a story of the many lives lived in the house. This museumization of Moshe's room is an attempt by the Rabbi to deliver a strong visual and affective message that terror is a crime against humanity. Events that unleash horrors and have the potential to bring about intergenerational human distress, injury and trauma must never be forgotten. They must never be repeated.

A large plaque has been erected on the building's roof listing the names of every person who lost their lives in the events of 26/11. The entire floor of the fifth level, where Rabbi Gavirel, his wife Rivka and son Moshe resided, was painted white to symbolize purity, innocence and divine benevolence as per the Jewish tradition.

What distinguishes the Chabad House memorial from other memorials in the city is that this memorial is one of the only memorials in the city that lists the names of all those who lost their lives in the multi-sited 26/11 terror attack. The other memorials are dedicated to those who lost their lives at a particular site. Through meticulous research and careful study of the various casualties at various sites of the attack, the memorial plaque at Chabad House is the only one of its kind in the city. Engraved on the wall in Mumbai's Chabad House are the words "a memorial to the past, testimony to a vibrant today". The Rabbi Israel Kozlovsky insists that it is a living memorial.

Apart from the plaque in Chabad House, there is also a commemorative plaque at the Oberoi-Trident Hotel that honours the survivors and victims of the occupants who lost their lives in the attacks. Seeped into a city's culture, these memorials become a representation of what can happen to people, to societies, to cities and the ways in which resistance persisted. The memorials become symbols and tools of human meaning-making for generations to come.

In the coming sections, we look at what the immediate response to the event was and its effects on international relations and the national community.

Security forces were deployed to Mumbai to contain the attack. The event resulted in the resignation of Home Minister Shivraj Patil, with P. Chidambaram taking over the portfolio. While 26/11 did not have the scale of public outrage that the assassination of PM Indira Gandhi had, nor the communal divide that the demolition of Babri Masjid created, it definitely painted India as a target for international acts of terrorism, which in this case was considered to be masterminded by the ISI, Pakistan's intelligence agency (Ahulwalia, 2018). The then opposition party, which was the Bharatiya Janata

Party (BJP), attacked the government's weak security policies. In response, the government amped up its efforts to improve security.

Official Governmental Response

There was a sharp wave of criticism that followed the wake of the event directed at the government. Newspaper editorials blasted the incompetence of the Congress-led government in handling such security risks. "Our politicians, fiddle as innocents die", read the Times of India headline, which condemned politicians and their game of politics in the wake of such a disaster. The BJP opposition used the event as grounds to garner a larger vote bank as the state elections were on the horizon. They condemned the Congress-led government as lacking the spine to carry out security reforms. Vir Sanghvi, a columnist for the Hindustan Times, condemned both the BJP and Congress, calling out their tactics of "using terrorism as an excuse to win votes". The Congress-led government began to undertake measures for security reform after the incident.

Coastal security was a prime target for reform, as the lax security measures had allowed the terrorists to enter the country undetected via sea routes (Ahulwalia, 2018). Singhal (2018), in an article for the Economic Times, highlights the measures taken by the Indian government to combat the ineptness of coastal security to deal with such threats. There was an overhaul of the coastal defence infrastructure and the emergence of a three-tier security arrangement involving the navy, coast guard and the marine police guarding India's near seas. The Coastal Security Scheme that was initiated in 2005 was expedited with greater funding allocations for coastal security infrastructure comprising police stations and radar stations along India's coastline. Despite all this, ten years later, the coastal security work is only half finished (Singhal, 2018).

There have been some successes, but the Comptroller and Auditor General of India (CAG) audit reports have reported that projects are lagging, and the majority of the allocated funds have been underutilized. The reasons pointed out for these discrepancies include a difference in priorities between the security bodies involved, i.e., the navy and the coastguard, and the lack of an apex body for managing the various maritime bodies involved in security duties. Currently, the National Committee for Strengthening Maritime and Coastal Security (NCSMCS) manages these bodies, but the management has been ad hoc and moderately effective at best. A bill to create a National Maritime Authority has been held up since 2013.

The policy changes included the incorporation of draconian laws within the Terrorism and Disruptive Activities Act 1985 (TADA), enacted after assassination of Prime Minister Indira Gandhi in 1984, and the Prevention of Terrorism Act (POTA), enacted by the National Democratic Alliance after the terrorist attack on Parliament in 2001 (Ahulwalia, 2018). Under POTA:

> Terrorism was redefined to include even political dissent against the government in power (as opposed to rebellion against the Union of India); the period for detention under trial was extended and the presumption of guilt was put on the accused.
>
> (Ahulwalia, 2018)

POTA was repealed by United Progressive Alliance (UPA) in 2004, led by Congress and TADA fell out in 1995. In 2008, the Unlawful Activities (Prevention) Act 1967 (UAPA) incorporated "draconian" aspects of TADA and POTA (Sen et al, 2015). This was the result of an amendment in 2008 following 26/11 (Unlawful Activities (Prevention) Amendment Act, 2008)

After these legislative changes, there were also increases in the capacity of the policing forces. Between 2009 and 2016, there has been a 25 per cent increase in the Union's special police cadres as opposed to an overall 3.5 per cent in its civilian employees (excluding the armed forces) (Unlawful Activities (Prevention) Amendment Act, 2008). The state government police establishments have seen a 51 per cent increase in the same period (Bureau of Police Research and Development data, 2017). These increases have been concentrated around conflict-affected zones such as Kashmir, Manipur, Nagaland, Mizoram, Jharkhand and Chhattisgarh (Ahulwalia, 2018). National Security Guard hubs were also increased across India to respond faster to threats ("Eleven years since 26/11 Mumbai terror attacks", 2019).

The most controversial change, however, was the creation of the National Investigation Agency (NIA). The NIA was formed by the Congress-led government to investigate acts of terrorism through the NIA Act. It brought under the agency's purview offences under several other Acts and several sections of the Indian Penal Code (Yamunan, 2020). The NIA is a central policing body, so the primary criticism it faced was the infringing of state sovereignty since police are on the list of subjects over which states have jurisdiction. The NIA is, like the Federal Bureau of Investigation in the US, a federal body that allows the Centre to investigate crimes despite the lack of a concept of federal crimes in India (Yamunan, 2020). The NIA can take over any crime that falls under the schedule of its Act. The NIA Act allows the NIA to act within a state without consent from the state, thus in violation of the federal principle enshrined within the Constitution (Yamunan, 2020). This, coupled with the mixed results provided by the NIA concerning terrorism-related incidents (Sharma, 2013) reveal why NIA is a controversial policing body in India.

International Relations and Community

The 2008 attack strained India-Pakistan ties to a considerable degree. This was due to the arrest of Ajmal Kasab and his subsequent interrogation by both the Indian Police and the FBI, which revealed that he was a Pakistani citizen and part of Lashkar-e-Taiba (LeT). His interrogation also provided valuable information, such as the attack being coordinated in real time from Karachi via mobile and internet telephony (Mahadevan, 2019). This provided a crucial lead in the form of a digital trail for the investigation team (Mahadevan, 2019). The investigations by both the American and Indian investigators also gathered evidence of the involvement of Pakistan's Inter-Services Intelligence (ISI) from testimonies of the apprehended criminals. Other than Kasab, David Headley, a Pakistani-American, arrested in relation to planning an attack on Denmark in 2009, was found to have provided intel for the attack on Mumbai. He also provided testimonies against the ISI and LeT. These facts, combined with Pakistan's refusal to admit that Kasab was a Pakistani national for 42 days after the incident, were the primary reasons for the breakdown in relations (Mahadevan, 2019).

After the admission, international pressure forced Pakistan to investigate. The Federal Investigation Agency (FIA), based on evidence provided by India and the US, had made arrests in relation to the attack. However, once the international pressure wore off, Pakistan's efforts slowed down, and at the end of the day, court trials were indefinitely prolonged (Mahadevan, 2019).

India believed that the attack was state-sponsored while the US accepted the Pakistan ISI chief Ahmed Shuja Pasha's narrative of rogue operatives in ISI having conducted the operation (Mahadevan, 2019). As of 2015, neither the LeT nor its front organization Jamaat ud Dawa (JuD) has been banned in Pakistan (Mahadevan, 2019).

The public discourse around the attack primarily comprised the above topics, i.e., security, the blame game and international relations with Pakistan. These are now synonymous with the official memory surrounding the event. India's border disputes and anger against Pakistan intensified after the event, and the Indian government has framed justice for the survivors as getting Pakistan to acknowledge and atone for this incident, something which Pakistan refuses to do ("Ten years of seeking justice for the victims of 26/11 Mumbai terror attacks", 2018).

This official memory has, however, allowed India to push for stricter security measures, and one such example is the NIA. The establishment of the NIA seems similar to the way hope was used to justify heavy security measures by the Obama administration post 9/11. There, the need to protect hope was used as the justification for the intrusive and draconian security measures. While it was never explicitly stated in this case, a similar vein of thought is not far-fetched. Hope seemed to have been used as a tool to legitimize the creation and continuation of the NIA despite its mixed results and seemingly unconstitutional authorities.

Post the events of 26/11, a new ecosystem of surveillance and security emerged. The National Investigation Agency (NIA) was set up through parliamentary processes. The NIA was provided with sweeping powers to investigate terror-related cases across the country and could override and supersede the police machinery of the state in suspected cases. Acts of terror such as bomb blasts, hijackings or attacks on nuclear installations were deemed acts against the unity and territorial sovereignty of India. Mr Chidambaram told the Rajya Sabha (while the NIA Act was being deliberated):

> People are looking at us. As I speak today, people are watching us. People will watch us on television tomorrow. People are asking, "Is this the Parliament of India the sentinel on TV? Is the Parliament of India an appropriate sentinel to guard our liberty?"
>
> (Routray, 2013, p. 49)

These two sentences have a commonality: they question the capability of the Indian government to protect the unity and liberty of India. This is a matter of both trust and hope. The word "hope" is not explicitly stated, but the implication is that the preservation of India necessitates the presence of the NIA, and this would allow for securing India's future and would enable people to continue to live, hopeful for their futures. This positions the Indian government and its security measures as the shield that is protecting the people's futures and, in turn their hopes. Despite the security rhetoric, it can be safely said that neither have the measures been effective nor have they even been competently enacted. Thus, the measures enacted and legitimized through hope have come to nothing.

This situation is interestingly like the truth commission in Sierra Leone. However, unlike Sierra Leone, in this case, the hope used to legitimize the institutions, are those of the rest of the population and not the survivors. This is simultaneously good and bad. It is good because the survivors have no promises being made to them that would inevitably lead to disappointment once the promises are broken. It is bad because rather than implement justice for survivors by aiding their recovery, the government uses the idea of hope to maintain the poor status quo that leaves survivors unable to recover. Hope is being used to speak of and protect a far more uncertain future rather than take actions to aid the present lives of the survivors.

The next aspect to be discussed is that of the blame game. The BJP-led opposition squarely put the blame on the Congress-led government. Their reasoning and the implications of it have been highlighted earlier. This is a serious problem in the aftermath of such events. The blame game takes attention away from the survivors, as parties are too busy trying to earn a vote bank. These narratives then get added into the official memory, once again taking away from the survivors' opportunity to cement their circumstances within the official memory.

The last key aspect that has been etched permanently into official memory was the involvement of Pakistan in the attacks. When considering the long and tumultuous history shared by these countries beginning with the Partition in 1947, this revelation dominated official memory. The emotional history between the two countries also helped justify the need for stricter security measures and India's stance on the international front against Pakistan. Years of discord also shaped the 'justice for victims' narrative as it became easy to deflect responsibilities of the state of India onto the survivors of 26/11 by blaming Pakistan rather than aiding the survivors.

All these discourses melded together to form the official memory. It thus becomes important to see how this official memory went on to affect the memorialization of the event. This will be explored in the following section.

Official Memory and Official Hope

For survivors, memorials and acts of memorialization serve as enduring reminders that sustain public attention and reinforce their pursuit of justice. In this section, we present the way memorialization of the 26/11 attacks as well as other key terror events has taken place. Below is a visual representation of the analysis of memorial events. The intent of this representation is to interrogate and demonstrate the people who have been the focus of these memorial events and commemorations. While civilians and survivors endured the most direct impact of the attacks, suffering egregious personal and material losses, public discourse has largely shifted away from their struggles for justice and compensation. The focus of remembrance has been shaped by nationalist sentiment.

Uniformed personnel, including members of the Mumbai Police and the National Security Guard (NSG), have been rightly honoured as martyrs, symbolizing national sacrifice. However, survivors remain largely overlooked, acknowledged primarily in narratives of cross-border terrorism rather than as individuals seeking justice, rehabilitation, or long-term support.

In order to identify memorial events and commemorations, a secondary data analysis using Google Reverse Image Search was employed. The intent was to scrutinize all images pertaining to major public tributes to 26/11 victims and survivors that received press coverage in English. The rationale for choosing press coverage of commemorations was to analyse media positionality that shapes socio-political discourse of remembrance events not just in India, but globally. The keywords used in the search include: *26/11 Terror Attack, Tribute, Homage, Mumbai, Candles, Victims, Remembering, Strength, Stories, The Taj, Chabad, Nariman House, CST.*

It was found that over a ten-year period between 2009 and 2019, there were 144 public tributes across 23 sites in the city; these were the commemorations that were covered by the English press. As shown in Figure 3.1, the images have been categorized under three groups: a) civilians or individuals referred to as commoners in public discourse; alternatively, those who are not part of the armed forces or constabulary practice, b) personnel or members of the police and armed forces. Those images categorized as "Personnel" include images where the term "martyr" appears and c) public figures includes political leaders (chief ministers, prime ministers, presidents), celebrities and individuals who are known to the public owing to their existing significant influence. Notable figures such as the Director of the Chabad Relief Fund, Anant Goenka (Executive Director, *The Indian Express*), the then Rabbis of Chabad, Baby Moshe (the surviving child of the Nariman House attack) and sites like the Air India building (where a laser tribute was held) are also classified under this category.

Memorialization of 26/11

Let us take a look at the memorialization events attributed to 26/11 and the focus of these events.

The circular timeline in Figure 3.2 visually depicts commemorative representations from 2009 to 2019, with figures symbolizing different categories. The inner doughnut depicts the distribution of 26/11 memorial events by year juxtaposed against the group represented in the event. The size of the group image represents how well they were represented in the memorial event. The inner pie represents the total number of events and is divided by the group represented. A clear trend emerges – civilian representations decline

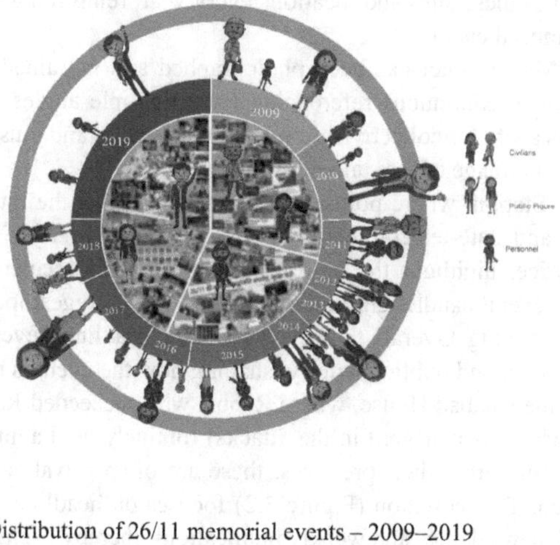

Figure 3.2 Distribution of 26/11 memorial events – 2009–2019

Source: Creative Credits – Ms Pritha Choudhury (Artist), Research Officer, TISS and Mr Kartikey Karnatak (Designer), Media Consultant, TISS

steadily across the years. The early years (2009–2011) show a stronger civilian presence, while the later years (2016–2019) are increasingly dominated by personnel and public figures. This suggests a gradual institutionalization of remembrance, with public memory shifting from collective mourning to state-led tributes.

The analysis reveals considerable institutional dominance in memorial events, wherein public figures and state authorities have presided over gatherings to commemorate uniformed personnel, whose memorialization has consistently outnumbered civilians. Over the years, personnel participation has been significantly higher, with peaks such as in 2018 (14 personnel, 4 civilians) and 2019 (13 personnel, 10 civilians). In contrast, civilian presence has been inconsistent, often absent in certain years like 2013, 2014 and 2016. This suggests that memorials are primarily state-led events, focusing on honouring official service rather than recognizing the grief and resilience of survivors and affected families. The prioritization of uniformed personnel in these events indicates structured, institutional remembrance that shapes public memory around national security and sacrifice, rather than the emotional and social trauma experienced by ordinary citizens. The sporadic inclusion of civilians highlights their marginalization in these commemorations, raising concerns about whose loss is officially recognized and how collective memory is being shaped by the state.

Between 2009 and 2019, most of these commemorations and public tributes primarily took place over 23 sites in the city. Overwhelmingly, the Gateway of India, the spaces in and around the iconic Taj Mahal Hotel, and the CST Station became the key sites, with a minimum of three tributes taking place at each of these sites and locations every year, reinforcing their significance in memorial events.

The Taj Mahal Hotel has been photographed and ingrained into public memory through continuous referencing from multiple angles. It has been showcased as a site for collectivization and mobilization and thus signifies its role as a central image of loss and mourning.

The CST Station, where police paid homage, reflects the intersection of public space and state-led commemorations. The Police Martyrs' Memorials, appearing twice, highlight the valorization of law enforcement sacrifices. Meanwhile, several candlelight vigils around the city suggest localized, citizen-driven mourning. Overall, the keywords in the headlines reveal a blend of state, institutional and public memory, shaping how the event is remembered spatially. In the Chabad House, where Rabbis who succeeded Rabbi Gavriel Holtzberg (who was martyred in the attacks) routinely held anniversaries of the 26/11 event within their premises, these are often private affairs or are not advertised. This collation (Figure 3.2) focuses on headlines and images from English news dailies and weekly publications, thereby excluding private tributes and personal social media posts. A clear distinction has been made between formal media memorial coverage and informal public tributes.

In the few years immediately after 26/11, the memorial events were focused on the civilians. This is important because, as we have seen earlier, terror events affect civilians the most. However, this focus has portrayed them as "victims" rather than "survivors", and this is an important distinction. Victims are people who have passed away and signify the survivors as dependents in need of charity. This allows governments to give them the bare minimum and, when asking for more, portrays the victims as "ungrateful". Survivors, on the other hand, are those who are picking up the pieces of their lives after the event and are thus people with agency who demand help to do so; not helping them is seen as "the government shirking responsibility". The term "victim" is what is widely used in narratives and thus becomes part of the official memory, allowing for the government to do only the bare minimum.

The term "victim" and its impact on memorialization is evident in the subsequent section. As the years rolled by, civilians became less and lesser of a focus in memorial events. Public figures such as politicians and celebrities became the focus, as well as the martyrs, rather than the survivors. The public figures focused on the martyrs as well as spoke of the injustices committed against India by Pakistan. This is evidenced below:

During the 10th anniversary celebration of 26/11, tributes poured in from politicians, and the State Government of Maharashtra organized a commemoration service at the Police Memorial in Mumbai and the Memorial at the Taj Hotel, Mumbai. The Chief Minister of Maharashtra and other diplomatic dignitaries were part of this event ("Ten years of seeking justice for the victims of 26/11 Mumbai terror attacks", 2018). The Prime Minster, President and External Affairs Minister expressed their solidarity with the victims in separate messages. On the 11th anniversary as well, the President, Prime Minister and other ministers, as well as Chief Ministers, paid tribute to the slain martyrs ("Tributes paid to martyrs on 11th anniversary of 26/11 attack", 2019).

While martyrs should be remembered, their memory is often used to justify the security measures to prevent such attacks in the future and serves to portray the state as competent in its response. Hope is being defined by the state through official memory. Official hope is often defined in terms of the protection of the hopes and futures of the citizens of the state. To ensure this protection, stringent security measures are often the way to go. Legislative measures such as the Unlawful Activities (Prevention) Amendment Act, 2008 and capacity building measures such as increasing the police force all serve this purpose. Hope and memory therefore become means of advancing state agendas that focus on security measures rather than the survivors of such terrible events. The official memory focused on martyrs, where justice is defined as trying to get Pakistan to atone for the event, contributes further to this narrative. Official hope, hope that is spread by the state, becomes a tool to propagate heavy security measures. This was observed in the case of the Obama administration as well (Wrangel, 2019). The 26/11 attack was another instance of hope being utilized as a biotechnology to create the "us" and "them" categorization depending on a person's relation to hope.

Official memory and official hope are thus linked by the fact that official memory serves as the narrative for official hope to take action to prevent such deaths in the future and to honour the brave men and women who had laid down their lives for us. With the official memory serving as the bedrock narrative, official hope in the form of hopes and futures of the citizens plays out in the form of heavy security measures. The flipside to this form of memorialization is that survivors slowly lose focus in memorial events and their words become less important to the public. This can lead to another problem, which is institutional indifference. This indifference can lead to neglect of survivors by local institutions. Another important aspect that stands out is the symbolic space used for the 10th-year memorials. The Police Memorial was not at a location that was directly affected by the event, and it is not an easily accessible location as it is within the Mumbai police headquarters. The other symbolic space associated with the attack is that of the Taj Palace Hotel. While this space was part of the attack, it is associated with the Taj Hotel. This creates an issue as the Taj Palace Hotel is a status symbol. It is a symbol of wealth and power and is therefore only accessible to those with economic, social and political power, which is something most survivors lack. The best symbolic space that could have been used was the Chhatrapati Shivaji Terminus (CST). Out of the nearly 170 people killed, 50 were shot at the CST and of the 300 wounded, 100 were injured at the CST. This makes CST the worst affected space in the attack. Despite this, CST was never chosen as a symbolic space. An accessible space that served to remind people of what they lost being disregarded in efforts to memorialize the event speaks volumes about the government's efforts to redirect people's attention towards the government's version of the event. If CST had been the space used for a memorial, people would have continued to remember the event and their losses long after it, which would have sparked their demands for justice. Without this symbol being prioritized, people's voices get curbed over time and they have no space to relive their memories, which would reinvigorate their hope to fight for a better future.

In the Naples case, we have seen the idea of "imperfect forgetting". This is like it. While the government is not actively destroying symbols of the event, it selectively remembers the event. The 'justice' that is sought is one of punishing Pakistan for its crimes. The people remembered are martyrs as well as faceless victims as they support the security narrative. The symbols chosen represent class barriers and, in a way, imply that some people are "worth remembering more". All these could be seen as an example of "imperfect forgetting". In this case, it is done so that people do not ask too many questions regarding incompetent governance and institutions. It also subdues people's voices demanding better recovery processes in the aftermath of terror events, allowing the government to maintain its ineffective status quo. All these actions and inactions by the state serve to highlight the poor memorialization efforts and imply a lack of effort by the state to understand what survivors truly need and what their idea of justice is. While 26/11 represents one case of memorialization in India, the memorialization of other terror events depicts an even grimmer reality for those affected by the events.

Memorialization of Other Terror Events

Now let us look at some other terror events that have taken place in India and how they compare with 26/11 in terms of memorialization. The following events were looked at for memorial events: Jaipur Blasts (2008), Ahmedabad Blasts (2008), Delhi Blasts (2008), Hyderabad Twin Blasts (2007), Pune Germany Bakery Blasts (2010), Delhi High Court Bombing (2011), Hyderabad Twin Blasts (2013), Delhi Bombings (2005) and Parliament Attacks (2001).

The outside doughnut in Figure 3.3 states the year of the event, the name of the event and the number of memorials for the terror event. The inside pie is distributed on the basis of the focus of the memorial event. The figure visually compares memorialization of major terror attacks in India between 2001 and 2013. The 2001 Parliament Attack stands out with the highest number of memorial references (14), indicating sustained institutional remembrance. In the Parliament Attack memorials, civilian presence is minimal, with visual space dominated by personnel and political figures, highlighting a formalized,

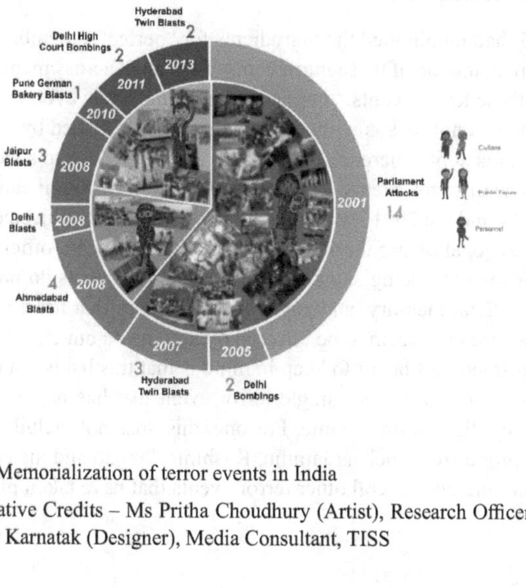

Figure 3.3 Memorialization of terror events in India

Source: Creative Credits – Ms Pritha Choudhury (Artist), Research Officer, TISS and Mr Kartikey Karnatak (Designer), Media Consultant, TISS

state-centric memory culture. In contrast, incidents like the Pune German Bakery and Delhi High Court bombings have fewer tributes but are dominated by civilian presence.

Upon a quick examination of the events, it is seen that most of the other memorial events were organized by the civilians and there was little or no involvement from the state in these events. The state was most involved in the 2001 Parliament Attack, organizing memorial events nearly every year since. Most of the other memorial events do not have an organized or formal nature to them and seem to appear sporadically with no semblance of uniformity.

The 2001 Parliament Attack, on the other hand, has received significant national attention. This is because the attack was portrayed as an attack on the state of India. All the people killed were labelled as martyrs and they continue to be remembered to this day, as their photos hang at the memorial erected for them in the Indian Parliament. The other attacks do not have such a narrative surrounding them. Three of the attacks – the Jaipur Blasts, Ahmedabad Blasts and the Delhi Blasts – occurred in the same year as 26/11. However, they have received little attention. A record of so many attacks in the official memory would result in many more questions regarding the efforts of the government and the "selective remembering" amongst the events.

The 2001 Parliament Attack also served another purpose: enacting stricter security measures. This was discussed in earlier sections. POTA, which was enacted by the National Democratic Alliance after the attack, has often been criticized for being draconian in nature. It was repealed a few years later.

Public Remembering

Tota (2005) had highlighted the ingredients for "perfect remembering". It can be seen here that none of these ingredients are present across memorialization efforts for these terror events. "Imperfect forgetting", however, is clearly present. But it does not feel as work-intensive as was described by Tota (2005). Instead, what is at play here is public apathy, primarily due to a lack of intensive coverage of terror events. The two events that have significant memorial events, 26/11 and the 2001 Parliament attacks, have been subjected to intense media coverage, allowing these events to have a significant official memory, despite this memory being skewed. The other terror events do not register a significant official memory, and any counter-memory that has emerged from these events does not seem to be covered by any media outlets.

Another important factor to keep in mind is that this list is not exhaustive; i.e. it does not include every single terror event that has happened in India within the highlighted time frame. For one, this does not include any events in conflict-prone areas such as Jammu, Kashmir, Punjab and the Northeast. It also does not include several other terror events that have taken place outside the conflict-prone areas, as they have not registered firmly in public memory for even a memorial.

There have been only civilian casualties across the listed terror events, except for 26/11 and the Parliament Attack. Thus, the martyr narrative is not possible here. The lack of martyrs tends to put a dent in the government's narratives regarding the need for national security by using martyrs as symbols to unite the country around such security discourses. Civilian casualties cannot serve that purpose but instead serve to highlight the inadequate support systems that the government has in place to take care of the survivors. Thus, they are portrayed as "faceless victims" whose justice can only be obtained by the state by punishing those responsible for the events.

In the cases in which memorials are present, they are in locations that are inaccessible due to class, social and political restrictions. The Parliament is the location for the martyrs of the Parliament Attack, but this is a location inaccessible to the families of the deceased. The families must therefore hold memorial events at different locations each year due to the inaccessibility of the formal memorial. In all these cases, the most marginalized have no way to access these memorials, so their current plight can neither be seen nor heard by the public.

The "memory crisis" that was highlighted earlier is on full display here. Since survivors' circumstances are not heard by the public, they are quite quickly forgotten. This results in public apathy as well as institutional indifference. Their plights not being remembered have serious consequences, especially for those who are amongst the most marginalized. Memorials, as we have discussed earlier, serve as beacons to remind people that justice is yet to be delivered for those affected. But justice is defined by the state, and the lack of access to memorials means that survivors' definitions of justice never reach the public. Institutions can thus neglect the survivors and their needs, as no one can question them, given that the survivors' voices are curbed and forgotten over time due to such poor memorialization.

An example of such institutional indifference is that of a mother and her son who had been heckled by government officials for approaching them for a job. The family had lost their breadwinner, and the eldest son was then given his father's job. However, the son succumbed to an illness five years later, and when the family asked if the job could be passed on to their younger son, it was denied. This is but one example.

Institutional apathy is not uncommon since governmental machinery is often overwhelmed with caseloads and various groups of survivors making claims on the state. Owing to such apathy, survivors lose out on crucial financial, social and psychological support needed for recovery. The bureaucracy might prioritize procedural efficiency over the urgency of survivors' needs. Poorly funded and understaffed departments may struggle to meet increasing and incessant demands, and employees may behave in a desensitized manner when overwhelmed with claims.

The nature of individual, collective, public and official memory shapes a narrative of resilience, without delving into the question of whether affected communities and groups have sufficient resources to build resilience and whether there are channels for grievance redress. The voices of survivors explored in this book provide evidence of the range of issues faced by them as they struggle to rebuild their lives. Those survivors who experience institutional apathy then individually and collectively develop "counter-memory" or a form of resistance to the dominant narrative propounded by mainstream institutional bodies. Counter-memory, therefore, becomes a significant device for a more nuanced understanding of history through the inclusion of diverse perspectives, experiences and forms of remembering. Survivor narratives explored in the following chapter will highlight the counter-memory that has evolved in the years after the horrific event.

Note

1 As quoted in *The Dictionary of Humorous Quotations*, edited by Evan Esar, Section: Georg Hegel, Quote Page 88, Bramhall House, New York.

References

Adorno, T. (1986). What does coming to terms with the Past mean? In G. Hartman (Ed.), *Bitburg in moral and political perspective.* (p. 117). Indiana University Press.

Ahmed, H. (2014). What is an 'official' memory? *Economic & Political Weekly Blog.* https://www.epw.in/blog/hilal-ahmed/what-official-memory.html

Ahulwalia. (2018). A decade later, is a 26/11 redux probable?. https://www.asianage.com/opinion/oped/251118/a-decade-later-is-a-2611-redux-probable.html

Barnagarwala, T. (2018, Retrieved 2023). *26/11, ten years later: Memorial and a new foundation.* Retrieved from The Indian Express: https://indianexpress.com/article/26-11/stories-of-strength/26-11-ten-years-later-mumbai-attacks-fadnavis-amitabh-bachchan-mumbai-police-nsg-5466112/

Bhandarwar, A. B., & Tayade, M. C. (2012). Mortality pattern of the 26/11 Mumbai terror attacks. *The Journal of Trauma and Acute Care Surgery*, *72*(5), 1329–1334. https://doi.org/10.1097/TA.0b013e31824da04f

Bose, D. (2011). Journalism caught in narrow nationalism: The India-Pakistan media war. *Reuters Institute Fellowship Paper, University of Oxford.*

Brockmeier, J. (2002). Remembering and forgetting: Narrative as cultural memory. *Culture & Psychology*, *8*(1), 15-43.

Bureau of Police Research and Development. (2017). Data on Police Organizations. https://bprd.nic.in/uploads/dopo/databook2017.pdf

Mahadevan, P. (2019, June 27). A Decade on from the 2008 Mumbai Attack: Reviewing the question of state-sponsorship. *International Centre for Counterterrorism.* https://icct.nl/publication/a-decade-on-from-the-2008-mumbai-attack-reviewing-the-question-of-state-sponsorship/

Pearlman, L.A., & Saakvitne, K.W. (1995). Trauma and the therapist: Countertransference and vicarious traumatization in psychotherapy W.W. Norton & Company.

Rai, A. K. (2000). Media at war: Issues and limitations. *Strategic Analysis: A Monthly Journal of the IDSA*, 24(9), 1–9.

Robben Island Museum. (Retrieved 2023). https://www.robben-island.org.za/

Routray, B. P. (2013). National security decision-making in India (No. 27). S. Rajaratnam School of International Studies. https://www.files.ethz.ch/isn/163172/Monograph27.pdf?utm_source=chatgpt.com

Sen, S., Das, R., Gupta, R., & Bhandari, V. (2015). Anti-terror Law in India: A Study of Statutes and Judgments, 2001-2014. Vidhi Centre for Legal Policy.

Sharma, A. (2013, March 3). Do we need the National Investigation Agency? *Economic Times.* https://economictimes.indiatimes.com/news/politics-and-nation/do-we-need-the-national-investigation-agency/articleshow/18768223.cms

Singhal, S. (2018). How this 16-year-old girl became a pillar for her family after 26/11. *The Better India.* https://www.thebetterindia.com/165228/26-11-mumbai-attacks-anjali-gupta-cst-station-news/

Stubblefield, T. (2015). *9/11 & the visual culture of disaster.* Indiana University Press.

Teltumbde, A. (2009). Capitalising on calamity: 26/11 and jingoist politics. Economic & Political Weekly, 44(50), 12–18.

The Unlawful Activities (Prevention) Amendment Act (2008). Act 35 of 2008 (Ind). https://www.mha.gov.in/sites/default/files/UAPA-1967_0.pdf

Tota, A. L. (2005). Terrorism and collective memories: Comparing Bologna, Naples and Madrid 11 March. *International Journal of Comparative Sociology, 46*(1-2), 55–78.

Tributes paid to martyrs on 11th anniversary of 26/11 attack. *The Hindu Business Line.* https://www.thehindubusinessline.com/news/tributes-paid-to-martyrs-on-11th-anniversary-of-2611-attack/article30084374.ece

Violi, P. (2017). Spaces of memory and trauma: A cultural semiotic perspective. In K. Bankov & P. Cobley (Eds.), Semiotics and its Masters (Vol. 1, pp. 185–204). De Gruyte, Berlin.

Wrangel, C. T. (2019). Biopolitics of hope and security: governing the future through US counterterrorism communications. *Globalizations, 16*(5), 664–677.

Yamunan, S. (2020). Explainer: Why Chhattisgarh has challenged the legality of the National Investigation Agency Act. *Scroll.* https://scroll.in/article/950225/explainer-why-chhattisgarh-has-challenged-the-legality-of-the-national-investigati

4 Hopelessness, Counter-Memory and Counter-Aspirations

The previous chapter captures the official and public memory of the event based on the analysis of the memorials, anniversary events and the official aspirations emerging from the review of the immediate response by the state and non-state actors. Chapter 3 also provides an understanding of the marginalization of the survivors in the macro socio-structural context, as illustrated by social and cultural studies of memorials, starting with Maurice Halbwachs' 1950 study of collective memory.

Memorial studies primarily focus on the various dimensions of memorialization like, for example, the collective nature of memorials, the complexities of memorialization, the role of memorials in fostering collective remembrance, community engagement and reflection, representation and inclusion in memorials, the memorialization of multidirectional memory, the politics of commemoration and historical and contemporary memorial practices (Young, 1994; Caruth, 1996; Sennett, 1977; Rothberg, 2009; Schneider, 2011; Braun, 1994; Doss, 2012). Thus, most memorial studies focus on the societal contestations over memory, identity, historical interpretations and representations. A subset of these studies focuses on the implications of the contestations around memorialization, upon collectives, in relation to the validation of loss and trauma, the psychological well-being of marginalized groups and community resilience (Young, 1994; Caruth, 1996; Rothberg, 2009).

The studies that focus on the therapeutic value of memorials, related cultural rituals and their significance for the healing process build on the philosophical grounding for the study of the significance of public spaces, provided by the early work of Hannah Arendt in 1958. These studies delve into the rituals and public remembrance (Arel, 2018), role in grieving process, facilitating mourning and community connections (Manderson, 2008), processing of individual narratives of trauma through collective memorials towards healing (Caruth, 1996), significance of public memorials for healing collective grief (Wagoner & de Luna, 2021), sense of closure and connections for those affected (Schaff, 2018), specific rituals to facilitate healing (Wagoner & de Luna, 2021), and case studies of individual healing facilitated by communal spaces of remembrance (Torres & Garcia-Hernandez, 2016). Though pertinent

DOI: 10.4324/9781003684954-4

in understanding the therapeutic values of memorials, not many of these studies had direct implications for interventions with survivors. The few 21st-century contemporary research efforts on mental health and memorialization that focused on the possibilities of online memorials (Walter, 2015), memorials as therapeutic spaces (McMillen et al., 2017), the process of creating localized community-based memorials as spaces of healing (Mwaura, 2011; McMillen et al., 2017) and representation of marginalized voices in memorialization (Henihan & Langness, 2019), were an exception. However, even these studies were focused on memorials and did not have direct implications for work with survivors. Thus, the impact of memorial studies from the social and cultural perspective remained at the periphery of mental health practice. This is especially true for India and the Global South, where the practice of memorialization/participation itself is a rare occurrence and a luxury accorded to very few incidents of terror, as illustrated in the previous chapter.

The psychological studies have dominated the therapeutic space, primarily focused on traumatic memories that are repressed, fragmented, distorted and dissociated among others, resulting in anxiety and depression. However, in a context where the health system is struggling even to provide access to basic psychotropic drugs to the one per cent of the most severely ill persons living with mental illness, access to individual therapeutic services following a terror attack is also a luxury. Moreover, the individualistic focus on survivors' trauma memory and resulting negative emotions, in total neglect of the context or only with cursory recognition, is problematic, especially in a context where recovery challenges are many and support services are negligible. The current chapter is an attempt to bridge this gap between social science explorations of the context and that of mental health practice by exploring alternative interventions at the collective and individual scale that acknowledge and address the implications of marginalized victim identity through appropriate support interventions and policy action. This chapter draws out these pragmatic possibilities from the narratives of the survivors and the analysis of their everyday lived and felt experiences. Though memory remains central, the focus in this chapter shifts from memorials to the everyday lived and felt experiences of terror attacks over 10 years. Thus, the current chapter explores the fluid memories, aspiration, hope, hopelessness, counter-memory and counter-aspirations shaped by the dynamic everyday context.

Survivor Memory, Hope and Aspiration

This section explores the memory, hope and aspirations of survivors emerging from their very narratives of lived and felt experiences, to be able to understand its interlinkages with the counter-memory and counter-aspirations that emerge over time. The memories surrounding 26/11 comprised vivid descriptions of the terror attack as experienced by the survivors, the pleasant memories of the past, the memories of pain and trauma and those of aspirations, all of which were fluid over time and space. The felt experience of hope and hopelessness among others was accessed from the tone, tempo, choice of words, the framing of narratives and the very expressions of felt experiences, which have largely been made inaccessible by the written structure of the book.

Memories of the Terror Attack: Most survivor encounters would begin with the narration of a detailed description of the terror attack, and the pattern continued until the tenth year. However, the content and emphasis emerged over time, shifting from detailed descriptions of injury and death to integrating more contextual details and reflections, along with the descriptions, over the years. Very rarely did the project team encounter discrepancies in the descriptions, which was primarily due to the disconnect between partial and complete in-depth descriptions.

For example – The survivor's description of the day of the terror attack initially revolved around her experience of being shot, waiting for support and hospitalization. However, several years after the attack, her request for back surgery was denied by the funder, as it was not attributed to the terror attack. In response to this denial, the survivor revealed that she fell off the structure used to transport her from the location of the incident to that of the ambulance and attributed her back pain to the very fall. Her hospital records corroborate this; however, the back issue was not addressed in the emergency and resulted in a slipped disc, according to the survivor. While recounting the line of events, she made a reference to the negligence of the laymen who didn't handle the patients properly in spite of their goodwill and the negligence of the treating doctors who prioritized life-saving interventions in the immediate aftermath.

Despite having repeatedly narrated the memories of the terror attack, the survivor would invariably start with a description of the event and its immediate direct impacts on self in a public forum, reiterating one's identity in relation to the attack. However, the one-to-one meetings at home or in the AAPTI field office would have rare references to the terror attack. There were also instances where survivors refused to share anything about their experiences on the day of the terror attack, even in the small group sessions organized immediately after the attack.

We do not want to share about the attack or anything that followed. We have narrated it to many, many people, including our own families, friends, neighbours and many others. We do not want to narrate it again. We would like to know what next? When will we be able to get back to work? Will we get our salaries till the hotel reopens? The same has been addressed through the large group meeting and we are re-assured by what we heard today. (26/11 Survivor Narrative a Week after the Attack)

Those who shared the experiences revealed in detail, including the time of the attack, what they witnessed, the nature of the injury, the things they witnessed while waiting for help, the initial experience of regaining consciousness at the hospital, the number of days of hospitalization and re-hospitalization and the nature of treatment received. The survivors from the families of the deceased often narrated the source of information about the attack, their ordeal of locating their loved ones, claiming bodies and their immediate felt experiences of numbness, shock, disbelief, among others. The emotional responses also varied with time and space, with the changing circumstances and context.

Pleasant Memories of the Past: The memories of the terror attack go beyond the descriptions of the day of the attack and are interspersed with or contrasted against the memory of life before the event, the memory of loved ones, the leisure, joy, travel, fun, health and wealth the family cherished at that moment before the event.

Box 4.1: 26/11 Survivor Narratives of Past Pleasant Memories

My child was a very responsible son. He used to take good care of us. He was not just a good son but a good brother who took care of his sisters, even got one of them married and cared for his niece and nephews too. (Elderly Mother of Deceased's 10th-Year Narrative)

We used to go out for parties, host parties, we used to travel to the village, we went to different temples. Life was beautiful then. (Wife of Injured Survivor's 10th-Year Narrative)

Life before 26/11 was beautiful. We used to go out, eat out, take children to the beach, fares, shopping… Now everything is inside this house (with her bedridden husband). (Wife of Injured Survivor's 10th-Year Narrative)

He was healthy and well built. But after the event his health deteriorated in front of my eyes each day. He loved to taste different nuts and fruits. Often, we hosted friends and relatives at home and cooked delicacies on all special occasions. But he couldn't even eat after the event. After his death we haven't even had a decent fast or celebration. God forbid, even my enemy shouldn't undergo such a fate. (Elderly Mother of Deceased's 10th-Year Narrative)

The above narratives illustrate how the temporal dimension of memory allows the past, present and future to exist together in memory and shape each other. Most survivors wanted to go back to the good old days of the past. They aspired to a better present and future, but when that seemed to be impossible, they wanted to settle for nothing less than their good old pre-terror attack situation. Those who managed to stabilize at the level of their past life resented their lack of progress, which the consequences of the terror attack hampered. Those who perceived a better present struggled to sustain it and take it forward into the future. These aspects of aspirations and their adjustment to the changing context are illustrated further by the narratives in the sections that follow.

Memories of Pain and Suffering: The memories of life after the disaster brought out pain and trauma as the key themes in relation to health, livelihood, self, family and others.

Box 4.2: Survivor Narratives of Painful Memories

Last two years has become very difficult especially because of health complications. Problems kept adding on. I had to leave the city to dodge money lenders, as they had taken my son away and threatened me to recover money. They also embarrassed and harassed my neighbours, forcing me to leave the city. *(*Injured Survivor's 10th-Year Narrative*)*

Due to my injury, I couldn't resume my previous job. I was into diamond polishing for a living and with my thumb being affected, I couldn't resume my previous job. In medical term it did not account for any disability, however I was fully incapacitated as I did not have any other skill other than that of diamond polishing, which is impossible without the thumb. Thus, running the household got difficult. We took up whatever work came our way. We packed sweets, made flowers and stuff like that, on piece rate. We worked all night as a family to keep things afloat. Still couldn't manage and had to pull out children from school and put them to work. (Injured Survivor's 10th-Year Narrative)

When I told my neighbour that I was going to attend an interview, she asked if it was with the Government for helping those below poverty line. I felt very bad. I don't deserve to be treated like this. I deliberately did not get into this situation. I had no other choice. (Injured Survivor's 10th-Year Narrative)

My expenses for the surgery and treatment were taken care of. But it took me 4 months to fully recover with the support of ongoing physiotherapy and other treatment. This cost me 300 to 400 INR per day. I am the only earning member and this created a lot of stress and related issues. (Injured Survivor's 10th-Year Narrative)

No one was there to stand by us. Even those whom we thought were our own, abandoned us after the event. If someone stood by us, we wouldn't have felt so lonely. (Wife of Deceased's 10th-Year Narrative)

These memories are situated within a context of poor institutional and informal support networks, resulting in desperate situations as captured by the narratives.

Memories of Survivor Aspirations and Hope: Mumbai is popularly known as the city of dreams. People from all walks of life migrate to Mumbai pursuing their dreams. Thus, migrants from within the state of Maharashtra and other states in India were represented in good numbers even among those who were injured and deceased in the terror attack. Some of the aspirations that brought the injured and the deceased to Mumbai are reflected in the narratives given below:

Box 4.3: 26/11 Survivor Narratives of Aspirations and Hope before the Terror Attack

We were doing good in the village. We were educated and owned land. But the education in our state is not good enough. Hence to be able to give good education to our child, my husband decided to go to Mumbai and start the "papad" business. (Wife of Deceased's 10th-Year Narrative)

My husband died in the terror attack when I was pregnant with my daughter. He wanted to put her in the convent school, such that she will have a bright future, unlike us. We were determined to work hard to be able to afford good education for our child. (Wife of Deceased's 10th-Year Narrative)

Aspirations varied from one individual to another, from time to time, depending on their economic condition, phase of family life, age, gender, residential status, among others. While men revered the jobs they did, parents cherished their children's success and homemakers took pride in their household contributions and valued their family lives, made possible through their contributions. The onslaught of the disaster challenged these little aspirations, and the minimum that the survivors aspired for was a return to the good old days. The realities of life in Mumbai also further shaped their aspirations for a home, stable income, better prospects, quality of life, among others. The following narratives capture a glimpse of these aspirations that had to be further adjusted to accommodate the fallout of the disaster.

Box 4.4: 26/11 Survivor Narratives of Aspirations and Hope – Varied and Dynamic

"I did all the household work and took good care of my four children and husband before the terror attack. My girls were safe, went to school and did well in studies". (Injured Survivor's 10th-Year Narrative)

I did multiple things to support my husband's earning before the attack. I sold eggs, clothes, taught Urdu to children and much more to make ends meet. I didn't have to ask my husband for anything. (Injured Survivor's 10th-Year Narrative)

Everyone wants a good life… today I too want my children to get a job, such that I can sit at home and relax… wants are never-ending… (Wife of Injured Survivor's 10th-Year Narrative)

In the immediate aftermath of the event, most survivors, though in a state of grief, mourning and healing, were very confident or hopeful about their future prospects, as evident in the narratives below.

Box 4.5: Survivor Narratives of Aspirations and Hope in the Immediate Aftermath of the Terror Attack

The people from the trust had come to visit. They promised to extend support for high-quality prosthetics that are very flexible. They told me that I will be able to walk like before and with that support I will be able to get back to life and work. Once I am back on my feet everything would fall in place. (Injured Survivor's Narrative Few Months After the Event)

After the disaster, I was badly injured and had to undergo amputation. My wife stood by my side and took good care of me. She pledged all her jewellery to arrange for the money to treat me. With her unwavering support and care, I felt hopeful about returning to my old life. (Injured Survivor's 1st-Year Narrative)

Everyone pitched in with support, immediately after the event. This gave me the confidence to move on with my life. (Wife of Deceased's 10th-Year Narrative)

As evident in the above narratives, the hope, in life after the disaster, was deeply connected with the small gestures of support extended by family, friends and institutions.

In the wake of such tragedy, survivors aspire for aid in alleviating their present difficult circumstances, towards upholding their future goals. Thus, that aid is necessary to keep their hope and aspirations alive. These aspirations may be a return to normalcy or a better future and they can range across a wide range of goods and services, both material and non-material, that the survivors require to move on with their lives.

Aspirations of survivors immediately after the disaster were often minimal and primarily involved returning to a state of normalcy or a state of familiarity. Thus, the aspirations from others were largely limited to healthcare services and support for sustenance in the immediate aftermath of the event until one could get back to normalcy. However, after the initial period of state-funded treatment, ex gratia support and altruism in the immediate context, hard realities of continued healthcare needs, loss of employment, cost of private treatment, challenges of disability, litigations or competing demands over ex gratia support, challenges of single parenting and disillusionment with prior aspirations, among others, dawned as the everyday realities of survivors. With limited rights and schemes available for terror survivors, survivors' aspirations for aid were often unmet by government and civil society machinery. This led to disillusionment and hopelessness, which the next section seeks to understand further.

Emergence of Hopelessness

This section explores the processes involved in the emergence of hopelessness, after the initial phase of solidarity, hope and aspirations exhibited by survivors. As the section above illustrates, the initial gestures of solidarity and support kept the spirits of the survivors up, resulting in hope and aspirations for a better present and future. With time, the denial of aspirations and hope led to the emergence of hopelessness, as captured in the narratives below.

Memories of Denial of Needs: The hope evident in the immediate aftermath of the event in response to the initial show of solidarity by family, friends, the state and the nation started to dwindle over time. The health issues of survivors and the death of the breadwinner cascaded into livelihood, education and economic concerns of the present, sabotaging future aspirations. The narratives below capture some of these instances of denial of hope:

Box 4.6: Survivor Narratives of Denial of Needs

The moment I refused to share the ex-gratia money with my family, everyone moved away, leaving me behind to fend for myself, with this meagre amount of 3 lakhs, for my entire life. (Wife of Deceased's 10th-Year Narrative)

I thought I would be able to resume work with my prosthetic legs, but it wasn't easy to navigate the Mumbai local train crowd, even in the compartments reserved for persons with disability. Thus, my ability to earn went for a toss. We lived in "chawls" with common toilets. I had to shift homes to find one on the ground floor with an attached toilet. I couldn't use the Indian toilets where you must squat. Hence had to spend from my pocket to construct a toilet that is accessible to someone like me. I couldn't travel by public transport and thus got restricted inside my home most of the time. Couldn't stay connected with friends and relatives in the village too by attending the key cultural and religious celebrations, as in the past. The prosthetic leg needs annual maintenance and repair. It must be fully replaced once in four years. I did not have the means to pay for the same. Hence, I replaced the flexible prosthetics with that of the Jaipur foot (the affordable prosthetic made in India). Thus, I had to readjust to the restricted mobility offered by my new prosthetic foot. (Injured Survivor's 10th-Year Narrative)

Everyone kept coming from ward counsellors to ministers during elections. Everyone made promises to support me. Elections have come and gone but nothing much has changed in my life. (Injured Survivor's 10th-Year Narrative)

Went and met the minister and he promised to give a job to my wife as she was educated. I kept sending applications but none of them were answered. (Injured Survivor's 10th-Year Narrative)

None of the officials had come down to see what was happening. Having heated debates in the parliament, that do not last for long, is not good enough, our day-to-day concerns will have to be addressed. (Injured Survivor's 10th-Year Narrative)

I have incurred the most disability (more than 80%). I went to all offices in BMC to ask for the shop space reserved for persons with disability. I have not got a positive response till date. (Injured Survivor's 10th-Year Narrative)

The crumbling of hope for recovery from the direct consequences to self, emerging from the terror event, among those with long-term recovery needs started becoming evident in the initial years after the disaster.

Memories of Denial of Future Aspirations: The denial of future aspirations by family, friends, organizations or the very difficult circumstances following the disaster was an assault, more painful than that of the disaster. Often, memories of the denied aspirations were expressed with intense emotions of anger, pain and sadness. These memories were not forgotten easily and stood out in the narratives ten years after the disaster. Some of these narratives of denied aspirations follow.

Box 4.7: Survivor Narratives of Denial of Future Aspirations

My injured son was in the hospital for one month. He couldn't walk, and I had to help him to even go to the toilet. The doctors forcefully discharged him against our multiple pleas. I took him to my daughter's house to care for him. She did everything from her side. Then we shifted him to a private hospital where they operated on him to remove the shrapnel from his leg. He did not heal properly. His wounds got infected. We took him back to the government hospital, but they refused to treat him. They would take him in when we insist and discharge him in a day or two. Finally, he succumbed to his injuries. (Elderly Mother of Deceased's 10th-Year Narrative)

An organization approached me for supporting my child's education to become an air conditioner and washing machine mechanic. I desired to make my son an engineer. They denied saying it was beyond my reach. My reach is much beyond. If I desire, I can achieve anything. I know what me and my family deserves? Because my children must equip themselves to support all of us and run the family in future. To be able to do this he needs good education… You are letting us down halfway saying what I desire is beyond my reach. How can I tell my child that its beyond my reach? Why can't you support my child's engineering education? Just because I am a victim of 26/11 can't I dream for a better future. If my husband was around, he too would have dreams for my son, like any other parent… I will work hard to realize my child's dreams. Will they not dream for a better future for their kids?… No one has the right to question my dream. (Injured Survivor's 10th-Year Narrative)

To fend for the family, after the attack, I decided to start working. Being a single working mother in the slums of Mumbai isn't easy. I cannot leave my girl child alone at home when I am not around. Hence, I had to leave my child with my mother. I had to separate from my daughter and that is my biggest loss. (Wife of Deceased's 10th-Year Narrative)

> Cost of living is too high. If someone is earning 10 to 15000 INR, from where he/she will save anything. My brothers were small, my child was small, my mother too was with me, with no other source of income. I am not a graduate to earn 20000–25000 INR. So, I got into the insurance sector where I will be able to earn as per my hard work. When the attack happened, I had just started working in Mumbai for 8000 to 10,000/-. I had to travel for 4 hours every day and work for eight to ten hours to earn this 8000 to 10,000. After the injury I was unable to cope with long hours of work and travel. Hence, I tried shifting my work by doing several beautician courses with the support of the trust. But freelancing in this field did not give me enough earnings to support my dependent family. I did not have the resources to start my own setup, and no one wanted to take the risk of supporting me with the initial investment. I want to educate my son such that he does not end up struggling like me in life in low-paying jobs. (Injured Survivor's 10th-Year Narrative)
>
> Immediately after the event everyone from family to relatives helped. But if I had received some support to run my family business or do any other job, I would have been independent by now. Now other family members are running my husband's business and I work as a labourer in the business, which my husband once owned. I am doing this to be in Mumbai and get my child educated in Mumbai. My husband left home and started this business in Mumbai to be able to have access to good education for our son. After the event we were left behind in the village. I was given an office job in Faridabad, after being trained in accounting software. It was my dream to be employed. But every other child in the family was studying in Mumbai. Hence, I decided to join the family business as a labourer to get my child educated in Mumbai. (Wife of Deceased's 10th-Year Narrative)

In the months and years after the event, the survivors encountered several setbacks on their road to recovery. While on their own these setbacks would have caused little harm, over time and due to deteriorating circumstances, these setbacks resulted in most survivors losing hope in the external entities (government and non-governmental organizations) capability to aid them in their recovery. Much like the situation in Sierra Leone (Ottendörfer, 2019), people began losing hope in the support machinery because of subpar government aid, bureaucratic pitfalls and inadequate NGO support.

The bureaucratic processes often took extensive sacrifices of time and effort on the part of the survivors who were simply trying to piece back together the remains of their shattered lives. They were often denied their due compensation because of "ineligibility", which was often arbitrarily decided by the officials who oversaw their cases. The lack of support resulted in the survivors' recovery being pushed back. Government oversight was also sorely lacking, as the government did not seem to care about the lives of the survivors beyond the one-time payment.

Box 4.8: 26/11 Survivor Narratives of Getting Lost and Denied Support

We had to run from pillar to post for receiving a sum of ₹3 lakhs. We had to reach out to the right people and give our identification proofs. Whereas, at that point in time we were not in the condition to do all these things. We went through this to ensure that our names were included in the list of people who would receive ex gratia from the government. The government gave us ₹3 lakhs as though it has done away with its responsibility once and for all. If only we felt that someone responsible was with us, we wouldn't have felt so helpless. (10th-Year Wife of the Deceased's Narrative)

I have maximum disability from among all the survivors of 26/11. I hired a lawyer to file the application for the terror survivors support scheme. My application was rejected, and I don't know why. (10th-Year Injured Survivor's Narrative)

We didn't know whom to approach, or where to go for information from the government. If only someone had stood by us or turned back to see how we were living or dead and gone, we would have felt much supported. (Wife of Deceased's 10th-Year Narrative)

Such neglect adds to the trauma of the losses that survivors have faced. Many survivors reported continued suffering from physical injury or mental distress. This often resulted in a feeling of helplessness. They encountered difficulties in facing their families, and the lack of government support compounded the issues. But it is not just the government that has abandoned them. Survivors also must deal with their relatives and neighbours treating them with disdain and indifference. The costs of treatment and the emerging needs of the survivors, due to physical and mental trauma, result in their relatives and larger families severing ties with them over time. This adds to their distress and furthers them along in their feelings of disillusionment and hopelessness. Denial of aspirations was not only about material support but also the denial of due recognition of loved one's contribution by formal stakeholders. The denial of recognition or the sense of contribution was not limited to the formal stakeholders but also a very everyday lived reality, as evident in the narratives below:

Box 4.9: 26/11 Survivors Narratives of Denial of Recognition for Contributions

The government had issued the order to present an award to my father, who passed away two years after the event due to health complications. My mother applied for the award, but we are yet to receive it. (Son of Deceased's 10th-Year Narrative)

I did all the household work and took good care of my four children and husband before the terror attack. My girls were safe, went to school and did well in studies. After the disaster, I went to multiple doctors and even underwent surgeries to get better. I am unable to do anything for the family. Now I just sit around and get my husband and children to do all the work. I have become a burden for them. (Injured Survivor's 10th-Year Narrative)

Before the attack, I never took money from my husband to run the family. I did multiple things to run the family. But now even to step out of the house, I need the support of my family. They are also tired of my health issues that have drained the family's finances and my dependence on them for even small things. Everyone has moved away including my siblings, my sons, their families. Even my husband's attitude towards me has changed… (Injured Survivor's 10th-Year Narrative)

The biggest difference in my life before and after the incident is that now I am dependent on others, am forced to live a life which I had never thought of. I can't do what I wanted to do. If I want to go out, I can't even do that on my own… I ask for help from all my family members. I must request them multiple times. (Injured Survivor's 10th-Year Narrative)

Immediately after the disaster, I was extremely happy to know that my husband survived. But now I really wish he was dead and gone, as I am unable to witness his pain and suffering. Along with him the family too is bound by his bed, caring for him day in and out. (Wife of Injured Survivor's 10th-Year Narrative)

After the disaster, I have failed in front of my children's eyes. What kind of a mother am I, who is unable to fulfil my children's basic necessities in life? I am sitting at home to care for my bedridden husband and not earning a penny to support my children's needs. (Wife of Injured Survivor's 10th-Year Narrative)

My wife came down to visit me in the hospital immediately after my amputation. Then she left and never returned. Later, I realized that she married another man. (Injured Survivor's 10th-Year Narrative)

> Before my wedding I have fought elections at my maternal village. I can't go back to my old days because of my injured leg. I know, I still have the strength to move forward in life. I have the talent and strength, but I need someone's help, only then I shall win and show it to India. (Injured Survivor's 10th-Year Narrative)

The argument being presented in this chapter is not that disillusionment and hopelessness are simply negative traits for survivors. Hopelessness leads to the formation of a counter-memory. This formation of the counter-memory can be both therapeutic and can result in survivors finding a new set of aspirations for the future based on their experiences. Rather than living a life of false hopes handed to them by the state/public institutions, survivors, through their hopelessness, have been able to form counter-memories and counter-aspirations that allow them to heal and get ready to act.

Survivors Counter-Memory

In the immediate aftermath, the survivors very often parroted the official memory of the event, in terms of security threats that were unforeseen, the sense of solidarity and their gratitude towards service providers, as evident in the following narratives:

> **Box 4.10: 26/11 Survivor Narratives that Aligned with the Official and Public Narrative**
>
> We received very good treatment; however bad the other services were. If not for the timely treatment, many of us would not have been alive today. (Injured Survivor's 1st-Year Narrative)
>
> I am thankful to the Hindu brother, who reached out to me in the hospital while I was being discharged. Though not of much support in terms of financial help, the solidarity and brotherhood extended is sincerely appreciated. (Injured Survivor's 10th-Year Narrative)
>
> No one would have foreseen such an incident (terror attack)... (Injured Survivor's 10th-Year Narrative)

There were counter-memories and aspirations in the public domain displayed as banners and placards as part of candlelight and solidarity marches, immediately after the event. These were from the public domain questioning the differential treatment of personnel, cricketers and civilians in terms of valour and compensation. Some of these counter-memories and aspirations were parroted by a few survivors in the initial months. These survivors were troubled by their emergency support and immediate relief inadequacies, especially when they hit a dead end regarding promised support. They hitched on to failed promises made in the immediate aftermath of the event, based on their experience of not receiving sufficient support for treatment and care. However, the counter-memories and aspirations that emerged from their everyday lived experiences, in the tenth-year narratives, were more widespread among the survivors.

The tenth-year narratives largely revealed the hardships and the counter-memory of the event, raising difficult questions about the security lapse, lapses in emergency services, medical negligence, disparities regarding compensation and support services, among others. These counter-memories emerged from the lived and felt experiences of interactions with government officials, non-governmental organizations, family, friends, neighbours and the world around them, after the incident, as illustrated in the narratives below:

Box 4.11: 26/11 Counter-Memory – 10th-Year Narratives

The government gave money just once and then forgot about us. It should not have been like this. Things should have been planned accordingly after understanding our needs. (Wife of Deceased's 10th-Year Narrative)

When VIPs visited the hospitals immediately after the incident, I was locked up in the MRI (Magnetic Resonnace Imaging) room repeatedly to prevent me from voicing our concerns to the visitors. I was locked up every time a VIP visit was scheduled. When I voiced the injured survivor's concerns of poor care and negligence to the media, they (Hospital Authorities) were focused on creating counter-narratives that sabotaged my stature, rather than addressing the concerns in care and treatment. (Injured Survivor's 1st & 10th-Year Narrative)

...What kind of security systems do we have in place? We didn't even realize that the terrorists were coming in? Isn't it (the nation) like our house with doors and safety measures in place? Unless someone from inside opens the door, how can the terrorist come in? Who opened the doors for them? How can we allow for such an incident to happen? ...(Injured Survivor's 10th-Year Narrative)

...First of all such incidents happen due to the carelessness of government systems and institutions... (Injured Survivor's 10th-Year Narrative)

...the most important of all is emergency services. I was injured at 9.30 pm and the ambulance came at around 11.00 pm, around one and half hours late. The pain and trauma that I had to endure, no one else should suffer. Few of the injured died within an hour, they could have been saved...(Injured Survivor's 10th-Year Narrative)

...I was given one injection to prevent the infection from spreading. I was conscious and sat there with the saline line in hand, counting 78 bodies being piled up. Not all among them were dead. Some were alive and could have been rescued if we had enough doctors around... (Injured Survivor's 10th-Year Narrative)

... for the same incident some got good compensation and jobs. In fact, most of them were in service and had good financial backing. But people like us only got 3 lakhs, and we didn't know how to take forward our entire life with the help of these 3 lakhs. To even claim the 3 lakhs, it was a big ordeal. We had to fill forms, get to the concerned office to submit it, prove our identities, provide other supporting documents. Our mental state was not conducive at that time (immediately after the loss), but we endured all of this to get our names enlisted for financial support, even amidst very difficult times... Many were not even aware of these processes; I have personally guided many...(Wife of Deceased's 10th-Year Narrative)

...whom to go to in the government, or which office to go to was not known. NGOs used to come to our homes and remained in contact with us and that helped... (Wife of Deceased's 10th-Year Narrative)

I got injured and lost consciousness. I was with my little daughter at the time of the attack. By the time I regained consciousness, my phone was switched off and did not know anything about my daughter. Neither did my family members know anything about me and my daughter... We were all worried for each other's welfare...until I could get re-united with my daughter and family...(Injured Survivor's 10th-Year Narrative)

...the job given to me (on compassionate grounds for the father's death) is like a piece of bread thrown at the dog... No one has returned to see how I am doing. I am being treated badly because I have made an entry on compassionate grounds... (Son of Deceased's 10th-Year Narrative)

... we were given 3 lakhs and left to struggle on our own... No one bothered to know and understand what is happening to us... if we were alive or not? if we were still struggling or have moved on in life? If our private employers were still supporting us? ... Every year the 26/11 anniversary was celebrated. Just taking interviews on that day isn't enough... Government should have looked back to enquire what happened to us... (Wife of Deceased's 10th-Year Narrative)

...even those whom we considered as our own moved away from us. I didn't have money even for his funeral expenses. His bank accounts were blocked ... I was left clueless with a 3.5 lakh loan and three elderlies to support along with my 10-year-old daughter. If only I had someone to stand by me and give me the courage to move ahead, I wouldn't have felt so helpless then... (Wife of Deceased's 10th-Year Narrative)

...timely and proper treatment could have prevented unwarranted disability. Delay in treatment has resulted in disability. People who could have been standing now have become bedridden. (Wife of Deceased's 10th-Year Narrative)

The counter-memories primarily revolve around the poor efforts by the government and other responsible stakeholders to aid the survivors, which has left them dependent on the people around them and thus robbing them of their identity, self-respect and dignity.

Survivors Counter-Aspirations

There is a need to separate the aspirations of survivors in the years after a terror event. This is necessary as the motivations for the aspirations differ over the years. Aspirations emerge in the immediate aftermath of an event and are often dependent on the aid of the state. The denial of these aspirations is what led to hopelessness. Counter-aspirations emerge from a place of hopelessness and with the aid of counter-memory. Counter-aspirations emerge from government and public negligence, which includes family and relatives. These counter-aspirations often consist of demands for changes in practices by the government, increased state accountability to terror victims, as well as calls for greater empathy from the public and family. Counter-aspirations also involve taking the necessary steps to restore their lives through aid that is given to the survivors by external agencies. The narratives below give a glimpse of these counter-aspirations that emerge from the lived experiences of denied hope, denied aspiration, hopelessness and counter-memory.

Box 4.12: 10th-Year Narratives of 26/11 Survivor's Counter-Aspirations – Better Surveillance and Emergency Services

... No one would have foreseen such an incident... But once it happens, the government must learn lessons to ensure that it doesn't happen again. They should increase the surveillance of vulnerable spots...

To ensure that no one else is injured and deceased in such repeated incidents… (Injured Survivor's 10th-Year Narrative)

… The government should ensure that adequate number of doctors are available at the treating hospitals. The government should be able to summon even private doctors if need be… (Injured Survivor's 10th-Year Narrative)

… Government should be more flexible with legal matters related to helping accident victims, such that onlookers will not hesitate to help the injured victim… (Injured Survivor's 10th-Year Narrative)

…the institutions in-charge of supplying medicines too should respond in a timely manner to make available those medicines and medical supplies that are not easily available in the market… (Injured Survivor's 10th-Year Narrative)

… There should be one department where we can go for all the information and submission of documents… (Injured Survivor's 10th-Year Narrative)

Box 4.13: 10th-Year Narratives of 26/11 Survivor's Counter-Aspirations – Better Health Services

…the injured victims should be given a victim identity card or a health card, with which the individual can get the needed treatment support, without having to make application, file supporting documents, take approval, incur the expense and then get reimbursed (the process followed by one of the Trusts to support medical treatment)… (Injured Survivor's 10th-Year Narrative)

…At this point in time I have been diagnosed with mental health issues. I am afraid of loud noises like that of auto or any other vehicle horn, traffic etc… I should be supported with health services that I need at this point in time… (Injured Survivor's 10th-Year Narrative)

…too much of attention was paid to the deceased… they are dead and gone… take care of their families, but also consider timely and appropriate treatment to the injured as a priority… they have their entire lives in front of them with families, children and jobs to be sustained…(Injured Survivor's 10th-Year Narrative)

…when someone is injured in an incident like this, they are often not from the same city. Thus, the injured need more support to ensure continuation of treatment. They incur expenses for stay, travel, sustenance and treatment cost, while being unable to work due to the injury and treatment. Some also must run families along with all this… (Injured Survivor's 10th-Year Narrative)

…Surgery and treatment expenses were reimbursed by the Trust… but what about the loss of pay, sustenance of family while being hospitalized, the expenses for restorative treatment such as physiotherapy for three to four months costing 300 to 400 Rs per day… all this needs to be considered in health support, especially when the injured is the only earning member… (Injured Survivor's 10th-Year Narrative)

…give the best of the best treatment to those who are injured. Everyone including the poor, irrespective of their ranks and status should get the best treatment as a priority… (Wife of the Deceased's 10th-Year Narrative)

Box 4.14: 10th-Year Narratives of 26/11 Survivor's Counter-Aspirations – Livelihood Support

…if we are given a job somewhere, everything will fall in place. If there are earnings, then everything else will be taken care of. You are respected and can live with dignity, only if you are earning. If earnings are not there, nothing is left behind… (Injured Survivor's 10th-Year Narrative)

…give me monthly sustenance, until I get back on my feet once again… (Injured Survivor's 10th-Year Narrative)

…the government, friends and relatives pitched in with money after my husband died… In some time, we were again alone… Instead, if we were helped to start a business or given a job, it would have been helpful for long-term sustenance and better for the family… (Wife of Deceased's 10th-Year Narrative)

…instead of the lump sum payment, if we were given money monthly for sustenance, life would have been much better… if the wife is educated a bit, if she could be employed then the family will be well taken care of in the long run… (Injured Survivor's 10th-Year Narrative)

…do not give me monthly sustenance… it's like alms to the beggar. I do not want to live a beggar's life… Give me a job, such that I can make a living and at least stand tall in front of my children, with dignity… (Wife of Injured Survivor's 10th-Year Narrative)

Box 4.15: 10th-Year Narratives of 26/11 Survivor's Counter-Aspirations – Housing Support

…you will have to extend schemes like the SRA (Slum Rehabilitation Authority) to victims of such attacks. Do not give us a house for free, make an initial down payment on our behalf and get us a place to stay. The remaining amount we shall pay as monthly instalments. Considering our economic background do not fix a high monthly instalment of 10 to 15,000/-. We are OK with a long repayment period of 20 to 25 years too…(Injured Survivor's 10th-Year Narrative)

There are so many schemes for housing. Extend one for us too where you do not have to give us a house for free. Make the down payment and get us a house. We shall do the monthly payments like how we pay the rent for 10–20 years. Or allow us to stay in any of the government quarters till we stabilize. (Injured Survivor's 10th-Year Narrative)

Give us interest-free loans through banks, such that we can repay reasonable EMI and own a house and have the hope that we too can live our lives. (Injured Survivor's 10th-Year Narrative)

Post such attacks extend us affordable housing, such as unoccupied government quarters, even barracks will do, where we have minimal facilities of electricity and water charges waved off… (Injured Survivor's 10th-Year Narrative)

…amidst very high cost of living, I couldn't manage to secure a house for myself. We are not asking for 100% financing from the government. Look at our economic situation and accordingly extend bank loans that are interest free… over the years we can pay back the actual amount, but it's the exorbitant interest that we cannot afford… (Injured Survivor's 10th-Year Narrative)

In Mumbai everyone dreams to have a house. If this accident wouldn't have happened, I would have managed to secure a house for my child… However small in a slum or a "chawl", I would have managed to get a house… (Injured Survivor's 10th-Year Narrative)

I have been in Mumbai for so many years. If not for this incident, I might have built a house for my child by now. Everyone comes to Mumbai with the desire to own a house. It might very well be in a chawl or slum, but still, we would have a roof over us. After the disaster, when we struggle to pay our rent, we are asked to leave, and we end up moving homes every second month. (Injured Survivor's 10th-Year Narrative)

Box 4.16: 10th-Year Narratives of 26/11 Survivor's Counter-Aspirations – *Inadequate and Inappropriate Support Services and Lack of Responsibility and Accountability*

...do proper enquiry and identify the most vulnerable families and extend support. See if there are old people, with only girls in the family and no other earning member. How will their homes run without support?... (Elderly Mother of Deceased's 10th-Year Narrative)

...my husband is bedridden since the incident. We incur a huge cost for his diapers, medicines and food expenses. His diapers cost 4500 INR per month, which is the cost of provisions of a middleclass family. His medicines cost 9000 INR per month. He is in this condition because of you (government not protecting its citizens from terror attack). Give me a nurse to care for him during the day to enable me to take up a job and make a living. Or give me a job where I can earn enough to support all these expenses incurred due to the attack... (Wife of Injured Survivor's 10th-Year Narrative)

I can't go back to my old days because of my injured leg. I know, I still have the strength to move forward in life. I have the talent and strength, but I need someone's help, only then I shall win and show it to India. (Injured Survivor's 10th-Year Narrative)

Many ministers promised so many things, but they never did give anything. I have spent ₹15 lakhs on my treatment, but what I got from the government was just 1.5 lac rupees. If the government supported us properly, I would have been standing today. (Injured Survivor's 10th-Year Narrative)

I have written to everyone. Governments have come and gone. I have approached everyone right from the local ward councillor to that of the Chief Minister and Prime Ministers. I am yet to receive any response. I would like to tell our Prime Minister, that we too are the citizens of this country... (Injured Survivor's 10th-Year Narrative)

If I would have got good treatment, I wouldn't have become dependent on my family now. It was all because of medical negligence and not receiving treatment on time. (Injured Survivor's 10th-Year Narrative)

The government paid the compensation and moved on as if it was not their responsibility. The people who were injured, what about them? How was treatment going on? Are they recovering? If they recovered, what about their life ahead? Can they work? How is the family running? No enquiry was made; this should have been done. Every year this 26/11 is considered and talked about but what about the help. Only taking interview on the day doesn't help. (Wife of Deceased's 10th-Year Narrative)

The government should aim at medical treatment, education of the children and after the education a job, this is my thinking. Everyone wants a good life, today I too want my children to get a job and my husband and I can sit at home and relax, wants are never-ending. (Wife of Injured Survivor's 10th-Year Narrative)

During this period if someone could stand with me then things could have been handled. Somebody who could just say. You are correct go ahead we are with you; it would have been a great support. Money is tricky, when it's there it creates problem, when it's not there even then it's a problem. (Wife of Deceased's 10th-Year Narrative)

Government should see that these incidents don't occur and even if it happens, the injured and deceased family requirements should be taken care of. If the bread winner is severely injured, the government should think about their family. If I am thinking like this that means all the people like us are going through the same situation like me. I think that if my situation gets better than before then its justice. After facing so much I would like a better life rather than the same life as before 26/11. I have faced so much since the incident, anyone will want a better living and to be much happier. (Wife of Deceased's 10th-Year Narrative)

The above narratives of counter-aspirations emerging from the survivors' lived and felt experiences highlight the core expectations from the state and service providers that are critical for recovery. Resonating with the themes of counter-memory, the counter-aspirations are centred around the need for better emergency services, immediate and long-term health services that are accessible and available to all in need, basic sustenance, livelihood and housing support. Survivors counter the narratives of aid dependence and misrepresentations by specifying processes that are to be put in place to assess the need and locate the most vulnerable. Thus, they resist the narrative of free handouts and base their counter-aspirations on concrete needs and challenges that could be objectively assessed and addressed. The last set of narratives highlighting the inadequate and inappropriate nature of available services and the demand for accountability and responsibility from the state stands out as the most dominant counter aspiration. Legal, procedural and institutional provisions to go beyond short-term and one-time support, with accountability and responsibility of the state, have been the key demands emerging from the survivors' narrative.

Emergence of Counter-Memory and Counter-Aspirations

The narratives by survivors indicated that they did not require endless monetary support. Instead, payment of bills, a satisfactory job and/or help with their children's education were things they wanted from the government. These counter-aspirations directed against the government and their living circumstances can galvanize the survivors to action. However, they would need resources to act for the betterment of their lives. This is where external agencies, such as trust funds, NGOs, public universities etc. can play a role. They can provide platforms for survivors to voice their counter-aspirations, to share their lived experiences with the government machinery and act upon the improvements that are necessary to aid survivors.

Counter-aspirations can serve as a means for survivors to navigate their reality. They can find other survivors with similar circumstances and counter-aspirations and form collectives that can aid them in their pursuit of "justice". Counter-aspirations formed as a result of hopelessness and counter-memory can serve as the foundation for survivors to act in order to improve their lives, and it is pertinent that external agencies seeking to aid survivors in the long term, especially in the absence of stable government aid, locate these counter-aspirations and assist the survivors in achieving them.

Having abandoned the aspirations to go back to the good life of the past, survivors started focusing on the future generation's education and jobs. However, this is not to say that resources are unnecessary to the survivors. The lack of government help and from their relatives would result in hopelessness and a counter-memory, but without aid from external agencies, this counter-memory will remain as a memory without action or simply begrudging acceptance; an acceptance that their circumstances will not change and therefore there is nothing they can do.

The argument being made here is that when survivors are denied their aspirations, it leads to hopelessness, which results in the formation of a counter-memory. The next step is the path towards either begrudging acceptance of their circumstances or the formation of counter-aspirations, and this depends on the availability of resources and support. It is also important to note that the availability of resources may allow for the change from begrudging acceptance to counter-aspirations. Once the counter-aspirations are set in place, the survivors can act with external agencies acting as facilitators, through the provision of a platform and resources, for the same.

Survivors' aspirations were largely centred around the return to normalcy, enabling a better future. The aspirations ranged across a wide range of goods and services, both material and non-material, that the survivors require to move on with their present lives without compromising prospects. However, the aspirations of survivors often vary from those of the state. The state's idea of goods and services tends to be unidimensional and universal. However, needs and wants vary across individual survivors. This leads to a dissonance between official and survivor aspirations, resulting in a state of disillusionment for the survivors.

Box 4.17: 26/11 Survivor Narratives – The Interface of Support and Counter-Aspirations

If it was not for the support from the Trust, I would have been left behind in a bad situation…. (Injured Survivor's 10th-Year Narrative)

The way we were supported with our children's education was very good. Many are illiterate. If support for education was not provided, the incident would have resulted in one more generation of girl child being left behind as illiterate…. (Wife of Deceased's 10th-Year Narrative)

I used to do agriculture before. I was supported to start a business of selling spare parts for the repair of tractors. This is better than giving money as sustenance, as I wouldn't have thought further and been at a loss when the sustenance stopped. My children's education was supported, and it helped a lot. My daughter was also given a job. All this helped me get over the impact of the event…. (Injured Survivor's 10th-Year Narrative)

I was a street vendor before the incident. I received support to gain skills to work in hotels. My life has risen from the streets to one of dignity and respect. My children are studying, and I am respected by my family and relatives. I have been able to deliver the responsibilities of a good son, husband and father…. (Injured Survivor's 10th-Year Narrative)

…many survivors were illiterate… If not supported for education, many children would have dropped out of school… like the illiterate parents, one more generation would have remained illiterate but for the support from the trust…" (Wife of Deceased's 10th-Year Narrative)

The state's failures to aid the survivors, as well as their narratives stating that they would, permeated throughout the lives of the survivors. This affected their interpersonal relations as well. Instead of solidarity, what some of them received was contempt. Since the narratives did not surround the survivors in the long run, public apathy towards them gradually grew over time.

Basically, as the above narratives illustrate, people wanted other forms of help that would allow them to reduce the burden on their economic resources that the event brought about. They did not wish for handouts or pity, just the aid that they deserved so that they could emerge from the incident towards the future.

> The government celebrates 26/11 every year. Just remembering the day won't solve any problems.
>
> (Injured Survivor's 10th-Year Narrative)

The above quote indicates the problem with the official memorial. Ideally, a memorial is a reminder of the need for justice for the survivors, and this justice is that of support services and packages that the survivors desperately need to get their lives back. However, as communicated in earlier chapters, the memorials do not remind the public about the fight for survivors' justice. Instead, it serves as a propaganda for the "justice" that is described by the government in terms of national security and sovereignty.

These practices lead to disillusionment amongst the survivors. This is like the hope leading to disillusionment observed in Sierra Leone amongst the survivors of the civil wars. After 26/11, survivors were promised long-term support by politicians and the government. However, this was quickly forgotten in the fight for "justice". This shattered the hopes of the people, leading to disillusionment and a counter-memory that highlighted the gaps in emergency services and the non-existence of any long-term recovery support services.

> Many ministers promised so many things, but they never did give anything. I have spent ₹15 lakhs on my treatment, but what I got from the government was just 1.5 lac rupees. If the government supported us properly, I would have been standing today.
>
> (Injured Survivor's 10th-Year Narrative)

There were many who were injured and did not receive proper treatment on time. Thus, they have lost their limbs or become physically and mentally impaired. This should not have happened. (Wife of Deceased's 10th-Year Narrative)

The above chain of events reveals that the experience of survivors begins with the event, followed by official channels narrating the event to serve their purposes, including promises being made to the survivors, which form the official memory. However, the promises are soon forgotten or rather subverted by co-opting the fight for "justice", and these, as well as poor institutional mechanisms for support for survivors, lead to institutional indifference and public apathy. These together lead the survivors to disillusionment and counter-memory.

While the counter-memory did evolve in the aftermath of the event, sadly it did not take root within the public sphere. This can be attributed to different factors. The insistence of the state to stick with the official memory and prevent the spread of the counter-memory is one factor. This is because the counter-memory accentuates the flaws of the government and their poor handling of the survivors' issues that emerged in the aftermath of the event.

Another factor would be the diffusive nature (as it is difficult to survive in the city without resources) of the Mumbai metropolis. People tend to move in and out of the city quite often, and several of the people who were impacted by the events were migrants who had come into the city looking for opportunities to work, educate their children or for other reasons. This results in people moving away from each other and not really converging together to share the counter-memory/aspirations or sustain the diverse efforts to converge in the long run. This would result in the diffusion of the counter-memory. The isolated survivors too would not be able to band together to force the counter-memory into the public sphere through protests and activism. The fragmentation of the memorials between different sub-groups of victims (Martyrs, Railway Station, Luxury Hotels, Police Gymkhana and Hospitals) and the lack of public access for people from all walks of life was another factor that contributed to the failure of counter-memory converging. The linear focus of the media from immediate impacts to that of recovery stories over the years came at the cost of denying any space for counter-aspirations and counter-memory in the public sphere. All these factors impede the transition of counter-memory into the public sphere, thus leaving the survivors and their circumstances in the dark/excluded from the public and state machineries.

This chain of events is, sadly, not an outlier in the Global South. This is the case in most terror events. The survivors are left without safety nets to break their fall while the government fights the "good fight for the people", and the fast-paced lives in modern society ensure that public apathy is simply a matter of time. The counter-aspirations emerging from the lived and felt experiences of the survivors clearly map the way forward in addressing distress and recovery among terror survivors. Better social protection safety nets need to be conceived to facilitate the survivors' differential recovery trajectories. In conclusion, the detailed case of Ms B is presented to illustrate how the various themes presented in this chapter manifest in a particular survivor's life as follows:

Box 4.18: Memory, Hope and Aspiration – Falling through the Cracks

Ms B was brought up in a church orphanage in Mumbai Central, run by the nuns. She didn't have any memory of her parents and family. According to one of the nuns (Sr. A) who was close to Ms B, since childhood she stood out from other kids in her looks, deeds and thoughts. Her fair complexion, curly hair, beautiful eyes and tall stature made the nuns assume an Anglo-Indian lineage. Sr. A remembered her as a quiet and adorable child who actively participated in all the church events and was thus the favourite of many. She was also remembered for her strong assertions – the first one in the home to detest wearing slippers to school and demand black shoes. She was curious about the outside world and expressed her desire to be out there to explore it. As mobility out of the home was restricted, Ms B, as a young adolescent, defied the home rules and ventured out, only to be caught by the security while sneaking in through the unused back gate of the church. She was angry about being punished as she didn't see the problem as hers, but one of institutional limitations. As she grew, her dreams, wants, assertions and protests also grew big with her. But she also knew that her dreams wouldn't come true within the four walls of the home. After 10th grade, she was trained to be a professional stenographer. Upon finding a job with a lawyer in Colaba, she moved out of the home to stay in a hostel close to work. Though she continued to visit the church, her friends and the nuns, with time, the frequency declined and completely stopped for about eight years, when no one from the home knew her whereabouts.

There are many versions of what happened in these eight years. Two narratives of Ms B – one to the AAPTI personnel and one to her newly found friend Ms Sudha, yet another survivor of 26/11, are as follows: According to the version shared with the AAPTI personnel, she married one of her colleagues at the age of 23, but it was an unsuccessful marriage as her husband was a drug addict. They got divorced 14 years ago (around the age of 46–50). Sustenance amount from the in-laws was denied. With the onslaught of computers, she couldn't continue to work as a stenographer, and thus started working as a tourist guide at Victoria Terminus (VT). As her English was good, she managed to earn 300 to 400 rupees every day. She had no place to stay after she got divorced as the home where she was raised also did not accept back their own girls after marriage. Thus, she carried a bag with her belongings and slept on VT station platforms. On 26/11, too, she was at VT station platform and she incurred a bullet injury.

As revealed to Sudha, while working for the lawyer in Colaba, Maria met her future husband at the Gymkhana Club. After seeing each other for some time, he proposed and Maria accepted. With this marriage to an affluent industrialist, not only did her long-held dream for a family materialize but also every other dream of affluence came true. After two years of marriage, Ms B desired to have joint ownership over her husband's property, which he refused, resulting in a strained relationship. Subsequently, her husband filed for divorce, and the marriage ended. Ms B returned to the church home and started working as a tourist guide, earning 300–400 rupees per day. Upon getting to know about her ex-husband's re-marriage, she had a heart attack and was admitted to St. Elizabeth Hospital. After discharge, she did not return to the home and started living at Chhatrapati Shivaji Terminus (CST), the earlier VT.

The two versions almost matched with regard to broad trajectories, except for certain mismatches concerning the reasons for the divorce and the timeline of the relationship and that of Ms B ending up on CST. However, according to the nun, Ms B started visiting the home again after a long break of eight years. The home learned about her marriage from one of her friends, as Ms B chose not to inform the home either about her wedding or the separation. During these visits, Ms B appeared to be disturbed and wanted to return to the home. As institutional norms did not permit this, the nuns arranged for a stay in Igatpuri, where she had a mental health breakdown for reasons unknown to them. After her hospitalization at Igatpuri, the home once again lost touch with Ms B. Reading the three versions together, one gets to understand the discontinuities and the situations that structured it differently.

The AAPTI personnel met her for the rapid needs assessment post 26/11. Ms B was admitted to St. George's Hospital after sustaining a bullet injury to her left leg and was later shifted to JJ Hospital, where she was treated for two months. This is where she befriended Sudha and moved into a Chawl room rented by Sudha for two months after being discharged from the hospital. However, she had to return to CST platform, as Sudha could not manage to retain the room due to financial constraints. Ms B visited the AAPTI office, and a monthly sustenance of 5000/- rupees was initiated, as she was unable to walk like before and work as a tourist guide. Though most survivors were hopeful of government and non-governmental support immediately after the attack, Ms B would challenge the meagre amount given to her by the government, comparing it with the payment that the cricketers drew, taking cues from the public narrative that demanded justice for survivors. Her long years of encounter with social interventionism might have been instrumental in her picking up the counter-narratives early on.

Long years of homelessness (roughly 14–25 years as per the different versions of her life narrative) and the 26/11 injury took a toll on Ms B's health. Post 26/11, she was not keeping well and was hospitalized frequently for breathing problems and swelling and pain in her injured leg. Ms B would visit the AAPTI field office regularly to collect her sustenance cheque, as she did not have an address (or a phone) to locate her. And it wasn't easy to get in touch with her unless she decided to show up. She would move around like any other homeless person with all her important belongings in a polythene bag and had her own reasons for not leaving the bag behind or not accepting a better arrangement. The reasons would always reflect her choice and assertion rather than the imperfections of the situation, reflecting her multiple self-assertions. For example, she would refuse to accept a replacement for the polythene bag, citing the earlier experience of having received a bag of dirty clothes laced with black magic, which brought bad luck with it. After two years when her sustenance was about to stop (as per the funders' logic of avoiding dependence), she was offered a job at the AAPTI office. She wasn't bothered about the discontinuation of her sustenance amount and didn't join, as she could neither travel for work nor wanted to shift out from CST. Though she lived on the platform, she was familiar with the area, had her own social networks and spaces where she would hang out and even play her favourite game of cards – rummy. It was a world that she had built for herself outside of the institution of destitute care and that of the family over the years and resented giving it up for any welfare handout in return. She guarded her freedom and choice, even under circumstances of dire need and deprivation.

Ms B had one more episode of acute chest pain with dyspnea (breathlessness) at the CST station, and Sudha assisted in admitting her to the hospital empanelled by the AAPTI project for the treatment of terror survivors. She was advised to rest and was on medication and was not in a state to be sent back to the CST station. As affordable temporary care arrangements were unavailable, Ms B moved in with Sudha for a few weeks and once again disappeared without any notice. Attempts to locate her at the station were also unsuccessful. After a few months of living in a hostel managed through her own networks, Ms B was again homeless as she had exhausted all her ex gratia amount received from the government and had not paid her rent for two months. Ms B once again arrived at the AAPTI office with Sudha, asserting her desire to restart her sustenance. Attempts were made to find an alternative care facility for her. Several old age homes (providing free and paid services) and hostels were approached, but none could accommodate her as she fell through their eligibility criteria of age, health status (without mental health conditions), mobility restrictions, work status etc. Either they accommodated individuals who were fully functional and capable of full-time work, or they catered to immobile, fully dependent older adults without mental health conditions. Ms B was in between and unwilling to surrender to institutional care this early, which she had detested since her childhood. Ms B's sense of self, entitlement and assertions, interpreted as symptoms of her mental illness or inappropriately pathologized as a mental health issue, also became a serious challenge in finding an alternative care facility. With several rounds of negotiation with the funders, the paperwork for settling her dues with the hostel and reinstating her sustenance was completed.

One of the hostels had agreed to accommodate her after 3 months at 6000/- rupees per month. Thus, the paperwork to increase her sustenance to 6000/- too was initiated. With persistent negotiation, an exception was made for Ms B for six months by paying her 6000/-, but that too was reverted to allow for uniformity and other administrative logic to prevail. Drawing from the so-called humanitarian best practices in Africa, the funders were unwilling to provide uninterrupted long-term sustenance for more than six months at a stretch. Pulling together the case of Ms B and several other older adults, and through a long-drawn negotiation process with the funders, the AAPTI project could put together the elderly pension programme to support those who needed long-term sustenance much later in 2014.

As Ms B cannot return to the hostel where her bills are still pending and with no other alternative care facility immediately available, she once again had to rely on her informal networks. Sudha was requested to accommodate Ms B as a paying guest, as she too was having financial struggles. However, this arrangement did not last for long. Ms B refused to pay Sudha and wanted to return to the hostel, where she could have an individual bath-attached room with a television set. As all negotiations with the hostel authorities to accommodate her at a subsidized cost failed and there was no scope for any further increase in the sustenance amount, Ms B had to return to the CST platform. Thus, all the above efforts could not keep Ms B away from the CST platform for long. In a few months' time, she landed at the AAPTI office in a very tattered state, both physically and mentally. She was hungry, angry and aggressive with her verbal assertions. In spite of informing her about the date when the cheque would be issued by the funder a week later, she visited the AAPTI office every day and persisted in her aggressive verbal assertions. Though the AAPTI personnel knew that the cheque alone was not the solution, Ms B did not rely on them for anything else. This time she was not amenable to any negotiations for alternative care and only insisted upon receiving her cheque, and as always, vanished out of AAPTI's reach upon receiving the cheque. A month later, the AAPTI personnel received the news about her demise at CST and the funeral at the very church where she was abandoned.

References

Arel, S. (2018). The power of place: Trauma recovery and memorialization. *Stellenbosch Theological Journal*, *4*(2), 15–32.

Arendt, H. (2019). *The human condition*. University of Chicago press. (Original Work Published in 1958).

Braun, R. (1994). The Holocaust and problems of historical representation. *History and Theory, 33*(2). 172–197. Available at https://www.researchgate.net/profile/Robert-Braun-7/publication/322757693_History_and_Theory_Braun/links/5a6edc160f7e9bd4ca6d948f/History-and-Theory-Braun.pdf. Accessed November 18, 2025.

Caruth, C. (1996). *Unclaimed experience*. John Hopkins University Press. Available at: http://ereserve.library.utah.edu/Annual/ECS/6950/Thompson/caruth.pdf

Doss, E. (2012). *Memorial mania: Public feeling in America*. University of Chicago Press.

Halbwachs, M. (2020). *The collective memory*. University of Chicago Press. (Original Work Published in 1950) Available at: https://d1wqtxts1xzle7.cloudfront.net/9579216/hawlbachsspace-libre.pdf?1390857178=&response-content-disposition=inline%3B+filename%3DHalbwachs_Coser_On_Collective_Memory.pdf&Expires=1746176425&Signature=cKlGNuE1Bim3lJRHKX4Jldl1Qoclk20Wz7si2kdDC6diH~RgMAbTlXDNOcFKh-cKKit2hUu-NLz9q34UIsm1Mk9bL2nFAXLImzw6RyAJXQAMZgVJZFq4UCiwKDp2WfwSSODfusaMNtJJnY7T990sIKiaoFLiwH0Fm0mtB8~HjG1Lds0xsW-jBHeOwUMcdppCILPFoU4VkiSrUpngJcdPwOS4CoXkno3VzeH6KrRrbS2l0Je9vb3ErMtLzoajZ4f~AlnGG3WPZglkHLJt0DYqvkSMb3FB0VMCsi8PNC8~KmLL7v0mUS9mgEmSEVEFlMFa3GRHPB7rz7ratzARpGIOVw__&Key-Pair-Id=APKAJLOHF5GGSLRBV4ZA. Accessed May 2, 2025.

Henihan, A., & Langness, M. (2019). Memorials matter: On the role of memorials in manipulating space to create places of racial reckoning. *Journey*, *3*, 25–34.

Manderson, L. (2008). Acts of remembrance: The power of memorial and the healing of indigenous Australia. *Adler Museum Bulletin*, *34*(2), 5–19.

McMillen, H. L., Campbell, L. K., & Svendsen, E. S. (2017). 'The power of living things': Living memorials as therapeutic landscapes. *Medicine Anthropology Theory*, *4*(1) 185–192.

Mwaura, M. W. (2011). *Community-based social healing approaches in South Africa: A case study of the Institute for Healing of Memories* (Doctoral dissertation, University of the Western Cape).

Ottendörfer, E. (2019). Assessing the role of hope in processes of transitional justice: mobilizing and disciplining victims in Sierra Leone's truth commission and reparations programme. *Globalizations*, *16*(5), 649–663.

Rothberg, M. (2009). Multidirectional memory and the universalization of the holocaust. In *Remembering the Holocaust: A Debate*, 123–134. Oxford University Press.

Schaff, P. (2018). Collaborative commemoration: Narratives as transactional memorials to heal the wounds of War and Trauma. *Military Behavioral Health*, *6*(2), 127–133.

Schneider, R. (2011). *Performing remains: Art and war in times of theatrical reenactment*. Routledge.

Sennett, R. (1977). *The fall of public man*. WW.

Torres, C., & García-Hernández, A. M. (2016). From violation to voice, from pain to protest: Healing and transforming unjust loss through the use of rituals and memorials. In Harris, D. L. & Bordere, T. C. (Eds.) *Handbook of social justice in loss and grief* (pp. 202–212). Routledge.

Wagoner, B., & de Luna, I. B. (2021). Collective grief: Mourning rituals, politics and memorial sites. In Køster, A. & Kofod, E. H. (Eds.) *Cultural, existential and phenomenological dimensions of grief experience* (pp. 197–213). Routledge.

Walter, T. (2015). New mourners, old mourners: Online memorial culture as a chapter in the history of mourning. *New Review of Hypermedia and Multimedia*, *21*(1–2), 10–24.

Young, J. E. (1994). *The texture of memory: Holocaust memorials and meaning*. Yale University Press.

5 Conclusion

Learning from the Everyday Lived and Felt Experiences of Survivors

The book acknowledges the social and cultural undertones that mediate traumatic experiences and views institutional processes and resulting injustice as traumatic experiences. It seeks to move away from therapeutic processes to address trauma, towards resistance-based processes by engaging with emotions considered "pathological", such as anger and grief, to understand the sense-making processes of the survivors. The book privileges the voices of the survivors and their demands for justice and transformation, which question recovery processes enacted by the state for the survivors. By privileging the voices of the survivors, the book seeks to highlight the efforts of dominant political discourses that pit perpetrators and survivors of terror events against each other in order to justify draconian counter-terrorism measures over the much-needed recovery measures that address the pain and suffering of the survivors of terror events.

Terrorism is a harrowing experience, both the event itself and everything that follows. We have seen in the first chapter how civilians are impacted the most by terror events and the processes leading to their marginalization. With these recognitions of impact and marginalization, the book focuses on memory, hope and aspirations of survivors in the aftermath of such events, as the conceptual framework to understand whether current policies and practices are just in their recovery efforts.

Following these conceptual explorations, the 26/11 event and its aftermath for the survivors were explored. It clearly brought out the skewed focus of the government on security. The terror event becomes a "window of opportunity" for both the opposition party politicians and the politicians in power to bring in peripheral agencies such as the NIA. After the 2001 Parliament Attack, the country witnessed how the POTA Act was introduced to increase security measures in the aftermath of the event. Such measures were possible because all narratives and discourses informing official memory portrayed the government and its security measures as "benevolent acts", intended to protect the hopes and futures of the state of India, which is synonymous with the hopes and futures of its citizens. The narratives and discourses also defined justice as forcing the state of Pakistan to acknowledge and atone for 26/11 and,

DOI: 10.4324/9781003684954-5

unfortunately, not hold the state accountable for its responsibilities towards the survivors of 26/11.

This official memory culminated in forming unidimensional and inaccessible memorials for the survivors of 26/11. Every year, the anniversary of the event is celebrated, but these anniversaries are skewed as they lack the recognition of those impacted the most by the event. Promises of aid and solidarity are made to the survivors by politicians, beginning from the days after the actual event and every anniversary that follows, as delineated in Chapters 3 and 4. However, these are overlooked over time, which further erodes the trust people have in the government and turns their hopes into disillusionment. The official memory facilitates public apathy and institutional indifference as it makes no mention of the most marginalized survivors and over time, only the martyrs and faceless victims are remembered.

The case for survivors of other terror events is even more dismal than the 26/11 survivors as the events themselves are not prominently featured in official memory for formal memorials or anniversary events. This is because most of these events, except for the 2001 Parliament Attack, do not serve the security and nationalist agenda.

All these lead to deeper disillusionment amongst the survivors, leading to the emergence of a counter-memory. This counter-memory is the voice of the survivors, and it is often neglected by official channels such as the media in their remembrance of 26/11.

The counter-memory then served as the ground for survivors who, aided by external agencies, were able to aspire to better lives leading to the formation of counter-aspirations. These counter-aspirations would serve as the basis for the survivors to take action to improve their lives, with minimal aid from the government, making use of their personal resources and those provided by external agencies sympathetic to their circumstances. However, this external aid is negligible and often beyond the capacity of one or two institutions to address as disasters including terror attacks are totalizing events that impact all dimensions of the survivors' lives. This further leads to bitter disillusionment, as they struggle to live up to the counter-aspirations that these external supports have instilled in them. Some of these agencies like the government and even NGOs set limits to the aspirations, which is often resisted by the survivors, leading to counter-aspirations and hope that primarily depend on self and solidarity with other survivors. These, when harnessed could lead to action initiated and led by survivors to serve their interests. We conclude with the hope for such collectivization as we document the hopelessness, counter-memory and counter-aspirations of the terror attack survivors.

It is the right of every individual in the nation to live a life of dignity. This applies across borders. The losses and grief endured during terror events should not cripple the futures of the survivors, and it is the responsibility of nation-states to ensure that it does not come to be. Unless this lesson is learned and passed on, the fight for justice for survivors will never truly end. Any state would be limited by its ability to address all the aspirations of survivors, especially in the low- and middle-income countries. What is required is a collaborative recovery process centred around the survivor, where multiple stakeholders come together mindful of the memory, hopes and aspirations of survivors in the design and delivery of the recovery process. A process where the survivors' self-representation in all phases of the recovery process is ensured; their voices recognized; and extends justice that is redistributive, taking into consideration their prior vulnerabilities and its implications for the spiraling secondary and tertiary consequences.

The key learnings emerging from the study that would support such a recovery process, which comprehensively connects all facets of the trauma experiences, from the macro socio-structural aspects to the everyday lives, are outlined below.

Invisible Survivors and Ineligible Rights: The Legal and Institutional Codification of the Official Memory

Chapter 1 illustrates the issue of invisible survivors, Chapter 3 captures the processes that result in the marginalization of civilian survivors and Chapter 4 demonstrates the implications of this marginalization for individual survivors and their recovery trajectories. This subsection on invisible survivors and ineligible rights further illustrates the marginalization of terror survivors within the existing legal and institutional frameworks.

The world has encountered terrorist attacks for a long time, and often the objective of these attacks is not limited to state actors and property damage but also includes innocent and helpless people (Meher & Shukla, 2017). Although most states have formulated counter-terrorism policies, there is no law or policy for rehabilitative measures for the victims of terrorist attacks (Meher & Shukla, 2017). The victims are soon forgotten due to a lack of restorative policies and substantive laws which provide compensation (Bajpai 1997), whereas the accused play an active role in the judicial proceedings with the criminal justice system constantly working to protect their rights. The fairness of the trial should also be seen from the perspective of the victims (*AG vs Shiv Kumar Yadav*, 2015), and they should be considered agents in the judicial proceedings instead of passive recipients being pushed to the background. The International Criminal Court, in the case of The Prosecutor vs Thomas Lubanga Dyilo, held that the victims also have every right to participate in the trial proceedings (*The Prosecutor v. Dyilo*, 2007). The Supreme Court of India has also stated that more attention should be devoted to victims of a crime (Meher & Shukla, 2017). Thus, restoration of the lives of victims should be a primary concern of the state apart from punishing the accused (Vasu Nair Rajan, 1981).

In India, although no definition exists for victims of terrorism, the meaning can be interpreted from Section (2w) of the Code of Criminal Procedure, 1973 and Section 2(k) of the Unlawful Activities (Prevention) Act, 1967 (Meher & Shukla, 2017). Hence, victims of terrorism are those persons who have suffered any loss or injury caused by the terrorists' attacks. One of the objectives of the Criminal Justice System is to provide justice to the victims of a crime (UN, 1985), and this can be in the form of awarding compensation. Yet, the question emerges whether compensation is the sole remedy (Meher and Shukla, 2017). In this context, the Hon'ble Orissa High Court in Saraswate Parabhai vs Grid Corp. of Orissa (*Saraswate Parabhai vs Grid Corp. of Orissa*, 1999), ruled that "It is the fact that perfect relief is barely possible, and money cannot make good a physical structure of that which has been battered and shattered". Thus, it emerges that though justice should be equal in value, it should not be alike (Meher & Shukla, 2017, p. 387).

Internationally, the United Nations adopted the "Declaration of Basic Principles of Justice for Victims of Crime and Abuse of Power" in 1985. This declaration constitutes a basic standard of treatment for the victims of crime. The Economic and Social Council (ECOSOC) has taken the initiative to implement the declaration, which involves helping the member states in accessing the current laws, instructing the officials, framing the compensation policies and encouraging academic research in the countries, among other things (Meher and Shukla, 2017). In 2006, the General Assembly formulated a Global Counter-Terrorism Strategy (UN, 2006), which seeks to "promote international solidarity in support of victims", and "the need to promote and protect the rights of victims of terrorism and their families and facilitate the normalization of their lives" and identifies the "dehumanization of victims of terrorism" as one of the key issues that generates the conditions conducive to the spread of terrorism (UN, 2016). In 2017, UN declared 19th August as International Day of Remembrance of and Tribute to the Victims of Terrorism.

In the Indian context, though the right to compensation is not directly enumerated, it has been recognized as an unwritten constitutional right (Meher & Shukla, 2017, p. 390). The Apex Court has analysed the real intention of Section 357 of the Code of Criminal Procedure, which empowers the Court to award compensation to the victims of crimes (*Sarwan Singh vs State of Punjab*, 1978). Earlier, the accused had to pay compensation, but in certain cases (like terrorist attacks), that is difficult and thus in 2008, the Indian Parliament incorporated the concept of compensation for the victims of crime under the Criminal Procedure Amendment Act, 2008 (Meher & Shukla, 2017). Due to this amendment in the CrPC, a new section was introduced, i.e., 375A which made it mandatory for the state governments to have a Scheme/Act for victims (Meher & Shukla, 2017). Yet, since there is no specific legislation for the rehabilitation of victims of terrorist attacks, attempts were made by legislators to formulate such a law, for example – "The Victims of Terrorism Bill, 2008" and "The Victims of Terrorism (Provision of Compensation and Welfare Measures) Bill in 2012". The Victims of Terrorism Bill, 2008 required the Government to form a rehabilitation package for victims by providing employment and vocational training, among others, and the Victims of Terrorism (Provision of Compensation and Welfare Measures) Bill in 2012 proposed for the Government to bear all expenses of the victims of terrorist attacks; however, none of these bills were passed as no further action was taken (Meher & Shukla, 2017).

In 2008, the Government of India approved an assistance scheme known as "The Central Scheme for Assistance to Civilian Victims/Family of Victims of Terrorist, Communal and Naxal Violence", which aimed to provide civilian victims (including their families) an amount of ₹3 lakhs only after a written application from the concerned person (MHA, 2010). The scheme was revised in 2016, with the assistance amount increased to ₹5 lakhs and the title changed to "Central Scheme for Assistance to Civilian Victims of Terrorist/ Communal/Left Wing Extremist, Cross Border Firing and Mine Blasts on Indian Territory" (MHA, 2019). In addition to the financial assistance, those permanently incapacitated and members of the families of the victims killed are entitled to a health card given by the District Health Society under the National Rural Health Mission, which entitles them to free medical treatment in respect of injuries and all other major illnesses caused due to violence. This scheme also provides for health care to the victims of terrorist attacks under the programme of the Health Ministry of India "Rashtriya Arogya Nidhi" and "National Trauma Care Project", which provides for financial assistance to patients who are living below the poverty line and are suffering from life-threatening diseases, to receive medical treatment at any of the super specialty hospitals/institutes or other Government hospitals (MHA, 2019). The children of the victims' families are also entitled to receive assistance under the "Project Assist" being implemented by the National Foundation for Communal Harmony of the Ministry of Home Affairs, which provides for financial assistance to children rendered orphaned or destitute (Meher & Shukla, 2017).

Yet, the scheme framed by the Central Government has not been adequate, and the victims find it difficult to get the benefits from the scheme because of the procedural loopholes and territorial applicability of the scheme. States have separate "State Victim Assistance Schemes" as well as those emerging from Section 357A. The nature of services and eligibility to receive aid vary across states.

Though there seems to be enough safeguards, the central and state schemes are application-based and have a limitation period. The central scheme has a limitation period of up to 3 years, while State schemes vary from 6 months to 3 years depending on the state. The eligibility for assistance and the amount is determined by state or district legal authorities, and this often leads to inadequate financial assistance or the outright rejection of applications citing lack of eligibility. There are also significant delays in receiving assistance, which is quite detrimental to the survivor's recovery. Another aspect to keep in mind is that financial assistance varies across individuals despite having similar losses, due to the final call being at the discretion of state or district legal authorities. Lastly, the State Victim Assistance Schemes have varied criteria and amounts of financial assistance depending on the state, which leads to lives being valued differently across states. The only common thread is that people's lives are undervalued across the states.

Of the survivors that the AAPTI project interacted with and worked with, only one injured survivor was aware of the Central and State Scheme for Assistance to Civilian Victims. Though she hired the services of a lawyer to make the application, her application was rejected at the district legal officers' level, without any explanation for the rejection. Often the ex gratia support extended after the event disqualifies survivors from benefiting or even making an application to the assistance scheme.

All these point to a need to move out of the current ex gratia support approach that is case-based and provide for a more rights-based comprehensive approach towards compensation that would allow for survivors to emerge stronger in the aftermath of such events. To understand the legal and institutional neglect further, we draw from the social science perspectives to delineate the social processes that result in the marginalization of civilian terror survivors within the legal and institutional framework.

Drawing from Agamben's conception of "Homo Sacer" (Agamben & Hiepko, 2002) and Mbembe's "Necropolitics" (Mbembe, 2006) this subsection illuminates the politics of life and death in the everyday post-terror attack recovery context of survivors. The concept of necropolitics, as developed by Achille Mbembe, explains how some lives are made secondary in certain socio-political contexts by the actions of governments, institutions and even non-state actors that align with the public narrative of the state. It often overlaps with the structures of marginalization inherent in a given context. The concept of necropolitics thus extends a perspective to understand the marginalization of survivors and their distress in the post-26/11 recovery context. The terror survivors' lived and felt experiences are located within the necropolitical landscapes created post the terror attack, to illuminate the differential vulnerability that certain groups of survivors experience. In Chapter 3, the study illustrates the processes that play out in shaping policies, public perceptions and actions to enhance security, resulting in the marginalization of survivors. The state mustered all its might together to fight the terrorist on 26/11, to save every life that was at stake in the fight against the nation's enemy. The loss of lives was not only heavily condemned, along with the resolve to seek justice, but also justified in terms of the unanticipated and unprecedented nature of the terror attack. However, the loss of lives among the injured months after the event during peacetime, for want of healthcare services, raises several questions regarding the resolve and solidarity demonstrated immediately after the attack at different levels across the country and beyond. The rhetoric of terrorism and nationalism was not limited to the official memory and media reporting (as reflected in Chapter 3) but also reflected in the narratives of terror survivors (as reflected in Chapter 4), revealing themes such as the need to alleviate fears, secure borders and increase surveillance by enhancing state control to prevent terror attacks. This illuminates the space where fear and sanction created by the terror event lend themselves to furthering state agendas, neglecting the survivors.

Understanding these zones of neglect and abandonment emerging within necropolitical landscapes illuminates the plight of survivors of terror. Past literature has largely focused on geographical or legal zones of abandonment and neglect (Lee, 2020). The current work takes it forward to illustrate how the zones of abandonment extend to psychic landscapes of fear and control, isolation, abandonment and neglect, until the level of individual survivors. The psychology of fear and security is used in certain ways to strengthen policies/politics of state control while neglecting the terror survivors' basic needs for recovery support, leading to abandonment without recourse. This abandonment without recourse spirals within the survivors, creating a state of hopelessness and despair. The study illustrates the emergence of counter-narratives of memory, aspirations and hope from this state of despair. Thus, the psychological distress experienced by the survivors cannot be attributed only to the trauma of the event and the individual survivors' psychological processes but to the political processes that unfold in the aftermath of a terror event. The swaying of public discourse is not limited to the dehumanizing of the terrorist, but also the valorizing of the martyrs, who only comprise the armed personnel and not the civilian survivors. The civilians thus get limited to mere statistics in most events. The book illustrates this neglect and abandonment of civilian survivors in Chapter 3 using the analysis of memorials across various terror events, which further illuminates the dynamics behind some events not warranting even a memorial, where the scope for security, nationalism and martyr framing are negligible. Thus, the book illuminates the larger political and social implications of the necropolitical landscapes of terrorism serving broader societal functions of legitimizing and consolidating state power during mass emergencies, resulting in the neglect and abandonment of survivors of terror. Membhe's conceptualization of state control, portrays a state that determines those worthy of life and death based on security assessments and priorities. This was evident in the way the state allocated resources for strengthening security and institutions for investigation instead of pursuing the welfare of the civilian survivors who did not fit the national security narrative as much as the armed personnel. Exploring the experiences of terror survivors through the lens of necropolitics reveals how power dynamics shape the public memory of the terror attack and its implications for the individual survivors.

Agamben's concept of "bare life – alive but stripped of rights" (Agamben & Hiepko, 2002), within the State of Exception, is being extended to the everyday long-term recovery context post 26/11, to illustrate the processes that result in the suffering and death of certain sections of the survivors, largely civilian. The attention towards saving as many lives as possible during the attack, the extension of immediate medical services and ex gratia support, in the absence of any universal right to assistance or compensation, operationalized to support the recovery needs of survivors, illustrates the manifestation of "bare life". The differential entitlements and support extended to different sub-groups based on the location of the attack (railway station, hospital, hotels and streets) and the status of the survivors (civilians, armed personnel, service personnel, employees – government and private, state of origin, among others), also illustrate the politics of life and death that systemically strips the rights of certain sub-groups of survivors. Historically, in the context of terrorism, survivors are invisible, and their rights have been overlooked against other national priorities such as security and sovereignty, as detailed in the first chapter and reflected in the narratives of survivors in Chapter 4. Thus, the death and suffering of certain sub-groups are overlooked or sidelined from the public discourse (narrative, perception, memory, aspiration, hope) in the wider interest of the state and its citizens. Thus, one reflects on the nature of citizenship of these lives that are reduced to a secondary status in the interest of the state and its citizens. The survivor narrative reminding the Prime Minister about them being citizens too reflects the agony of the secondary status realized in the post 26/11 context.

"We would want to tell the PM that we too are citizens of this country, and our plight too needs to be looked into" (10th-Year Narrative of Injured Survivor).

The initial co-option in the immediate context of the terror attack and the later sidelining of survivor voices in the recovery context, by the political discourse at all levels (in a context of complete absence of rights and support systems), leaves behind a sense of abandonment and resentment among survivors, pushing them to then voice counter-memories and aspirations of what transpired in their everyday lives since the attack. Though survivors resented being remembered only during the anniversaries and later being totally forgotten, there were very limited spaces within the public discourse to voice out their lived experiences of abandonment and resist the process of being reduced to the status of "bare life". The absence of universal rights, limited scope of existing assistance schemes, differential access and ambiguities within the existing policies and programmes for the support of survivors created landscapes of "bare life". This often blurred the boundaries of inclusion and exclusion, leaving the survivors at the mercy of differential interpretation and discretion of individuals interpreting the institutional and policy frameworks of the state and even that of the non-state actors. The legal status of survivors and their eligibility for many of these services was ambiguous, requiring the survivors to constantly negotiate their victim identity between the axis of eligible and ineligible. Agamben's idea of blurred lines between inclusion and exclusion and the concept of "Bare Life" thus provides an understanding of the lived and felt experiences of terror survivors, illustrating how they negotiate the interface of the state, law, policies, programmes, bureaucracy, media, etc. and their own self especially in terms of memory, aspiration and hope in the post-terror attack context.

The book also illustrates how State responses, or their absence, further aggravates the psychological distress of survivors by ignoring their support needs post 26/11. The survivors were largely seen as subjects of rescue, emergency support services and as spectacles at memorials in the initial years and did not have any space to engage in rights discourses, or rather the absence of them. They largely served the purpose of reinforcing state and non-state actors' narratives of justice and purpose in public events, resulting in disillusionment among survivors as their stories and support needs were not heard or even voiced. The survivors were intimidated by the expanse of the state and by not knowing where to go and whom to approach, as there were no mechanisms for access to the state machinery, illustrating the power differentials between the individual survivor and the state. Thus, the systemic abandonment and neglect furthered the suffering of survivors, as their support needs were superseded by security priorities. The marginalized identities of survivors, overlapping with the dehumanizing official narratives that shaped public perception, further marginalized these sub-groups. Furthermore, the dehumanizing of terrorists and their Muslim identity marginalized some of the survivors based on their religious identity. These survivors had to actively co-opt the public narrative and prove their solidarity with the state in framing their request for support. They also became cognizant of having to distance themselves from the identities of the terrorists and specifically acknowledge even the not-so-helpful support extended by individuals representing other identities.

> I would like to acknowledge the solidarity extended by my Hindu Brother, whom I saw when I got discharged from Sion Hospital after my surgery. Though not helpful in financial terms, I would like to acknowledge the solidarity extended by all.
>
> (10th-Year Injured Survivor's Narrative)

However, when their requests did not materialize even after ten years, survivors' counter-memory and counter-aspirations make vehement assertions of their citizenship status. They question some of these underlying prejudices based on sub-group identities, while reflecting to understand one's differential vulnerability and recovery trajectories. Thus, the book brings forth the significance of the historical, political and social context in understanding psychological distress, which cannot be described only in terms of exposure and impact but needs to be comprehensively understood by bringing together the politics of power, control, life and death.

Though we draw from Agamben and Mbembe to understand the marginalization of terror survivors and its psychological implications for individual terror survivors, the critiques of these perspectives (Owens, 2009; Walby, 2021) moves our attention towards social democratic principles and processes that lend themselves to pragmatic solutions to the problem in hand, in the context of neoliberal governance transitions. The strengthening of social welfare safety nets, universal healthcare, public infrastructure, inclusive planning and governance processes, among others, are the alternatives proposed to overcome the systemic inequalities and barriers in the context of terror attacks (Walby, 2021). Pragmatic collective and community-based solutions led by the state and built upon the values of equity, solidarity and public interest and well-being are proposed as alternatives to the resource constraints of the Global South.

The Material and the Immaterial Facets of Trauma Recovery

PTSD-focused studies of trauma have been criticized over the years for their lack of focus on the socio-political and cultural contexts of trauma, their event-centric diagnostic and therapeutic orientation and its inadequate understanding of the role of everyday stressors in the persisting emotional distress of trauma survivors (Ventevogel et al., 2019). Considering these criticisms, which have built over the years, mental health practice has sought different ways to address these concerns.

Psychosocial First Aid (PFA) has emerged as a practice to better aid trauma survivors. PFA was suggested as an alternative to psychological debriefing by the Inter-Agency Standing Committee and was adopted by the WHO (Zimmermann, 2016). PFA includes listening, comforting, aiding, networking and practical support with basic needs. However, PFA is currently treated as a solution to all issues emerging from trauma, with little to no context-based interventions being considered (Zimmermann, 2016). The tendency to universalize solutions to trauma is especially problematic in the case of mass violence, as it ignores every other problem emerging from the context, despite the effort to be more compassionate. PFA does little to ensure the recovery of trauma-affected individuals who need practical aid in the short and long term and are exposed to everyday stressors that exacerbate their condition.

Socio-cultural theories of trauma, on the other hand, take up an alternative ontological position focused on removing the mind/world duality which informs PTSD studies. They instead attempt to understand the contexts of trauma and the influence they have on trauma and re-traumatizing individuals. This ontological position has offered remarkable insights into the socio-political influences on trauma, everyday stressors and material realities of trauma survivors. In the case of displaced populations, Theisen-Womersley (2021) identified complex legal and medical systems as having significant impacts on the mental health of the displaced communities. However, this is overlooked due to excessive focus on the displacement event as the causal factor. In the case of terror survivors, Farber (2024) highlights the mental tax of the legal and medical systems as well as the mental strain on survivors fighting for compensation. Furthermore, the trauma of the event can not only strain social networks and interpersonal bonds of the survivors but can also serve to activate bonds of solidarity and support in some cases (Farber, 2024).

These studies represent a significant departure from the PTSD studies but at the same time continue to fail in certain regards. An important contribution of socio-cultural studies on trauma is that of discouraging the pathologizing of normal emotional responses and feelings such as anger and disillusionment which emerge due to the contextual realities after a traumatic event. But despite this contribution, socio-cultural studies on trauma attribute the emergence of agency in the long term to hope and resilience without examining the role of emotions and feelings, such as anger and disillusionment, in the formation of agency. Theisen-Womersley (2021) has highlighted the role suffering can have in bringing together communities, but again, is focused on how these can lead to positive relationships and growth.

Some memorial-related studies, on the other hand, highlight how anger and disillusionment can lead to agency as people take the matter of memorialization into their own hands, highlighting the role of these emotions and feelings in the development of agency (Tota, 2005; Toribio Medina 2024). But these studies focus exclusively on memorials without looking at the other contributions that this anger and disillusionment can result in, such as the formation of counter-aspirations among individuals. By focusing on agency and material rights, this subsection highlights how these ideas are co-constitutive. To understand this, there is a need to first understand how agency has been studied at present in the case of terror survivors.

Agency has been a topic of discussion to understand the experiences of terror survivors in the aftermath of terror events. This discussion has been limited without adequate focus on how the larger material world interfaces with the agency of individuals (Farber, 2024) and the range of emotions and feelings, such as anger and disillusionment, that influence agency.

Another emergent discussion considers how media portrayal of survivors affects the meaning-making process of the public regarding the survivors and the event (Wesley, 2024). One aspect is the cultural context and power structures in different societies that affects how survivors are portrayed by the media, and this in turn, can impact individuals' autonomy and ability to define their experiences with terror events (Wesley, 2024). However, there is little discussion regarding how survivors can reclaim their agency, which is curbed by these portrayals. This discussion does bring up the cultural context and its influence on media portrayal, with apparent differences in the US and Nigeria due to the respective individualist and collectivist societies (Wesley, 2024).

The discussions on materiality and agency primarily involve space, specifically memorial spaces and the embodiment of trauma. The design and discourse around memorial spaces serve to include and alienate various groups of people (García González, 2019). Who is included and who is not? The excluded groups will lose the space to process their trauma and make sense of what they experienced. However, studies argue that it would be reductive to look at memorial spaces as rigid spaces; instead, they need to be seen as spaces in "permanent flux" (Jirku & Sánchez-Biosca, 2021 as cited in Vollmeyer, 2023). This presents memorial spaces as material spaces that offer reprieve from distress, and exclusion from these spaces can result in people attempting to retake these spaces, an assertion of their agency to be precise.

Embodiment is the next dimension of the materiality-agency interface. The body is seen as the material site that interacts with the world, and trauma can disrupt and detach the body from the world (Liebig, 2019; Malabou, 2012). The embodiment perspective has been used extensively to understand the material effects of trauma and, specifically, terrorism on its survivors. The perspective veers from the psychological focus of trauma, allowing one to view and understand perspectives such as detachment, the impacts of physical injuries and bodily aftershocks of a traumatic event (Liebig, 2019).

However, despite these insights, there have been few works in terrorism-related literature that have moved beyond these conceptions. The few studies that have emerged over recent years, investigated media portrayals of terror survivors and the impact this has on their agency (Wesley, 2024) and others have looked at the context in which terror survivors lived after the event (Farber, 2024; Yanay & Gal, 2010; Farber & Benichou, 2021). This highlighted issues with the legal system, survivors highlighting their lack of voice, the re-traumatizing effects of the legal process and the perception of these systems as prioritizing the rights of terrorists over the survivors. Next, it highlights the practical challenges and injustices of the compensation schemes, financial strains due to medical bills and lost incomes and the effects of injuries and physical disabilities caused by the terror event. These aspects are highlighted as fundamental to our own study and are treated as part of the material world that affects the agency of terror survivors. However, what more has emerged from our work are the crucial roles of emotions and feelings, such as anger and disillusionment, and how they propel the survivors' counter-aspirations around the constraints of their everyday world. Thus, the study moves away from "positive" emotions and feelings such as hope and resilience and acknowledges the material constraints on agency and how survivors navigate these constraints. This adds a key dimension to the co-constitutive nature of materialism and agency, a key contribution of the book.

The portrayal of agency as an inherent quality within individuals is further challenged within this study. This view of agency is concerning as it pushes the onus of recovery onto the survivors. This allows for denial of compensation, unjust bureaucratic processes and indifference about the plight of survivors by the public to be accepted as the norm. The denial of material rights stunts the agency of the survivors as they are left unable to exert their agency in the traditional sense due to the burdens placed on them to recover from their horrific experience. In this situation, agency is unlikely to be built on feelings and emotions of hope and resilience, as the burdens of reality and the broken promises instead cause the emergence of emotions and feelings of anger and disillusionment. Ironically, the denial of material rights results in an agency built on anger and hopelessness, an agency for resistance. This agency allows communities to resist the current systems of denied compensation, unjust bureaucracies, broken promises and public indifference and forgetfulness. They assert alternative trajectories of recovery that move away from conceptions of universal individual recovery towards recovery processes situated within their own realities.

Alongside these reasons, memorial events play a crucial role in the building of this agency of resistance. Memorial spaces are material spaces, as highlighted by other studies, which allow survivors to process their memories and emotions surrounding the event. However, the trends observed in this study indicate a slow exclusion of large groups of communities from these memorial spaces, which curbs their voices, their stories and results in stifling their agency. These experiences are channelled into the formation of counter-memories and counter-aspirations which further the agency for resistance.

Counter-aspirations present a case for an agency of resistance quite clearly. The aspirations voiced by the survivors focus heavily on grounded material and non-material needs. Counter-aspirations emerge because of the inadequate compensation, support and broken social networks and thus focus on addressing the emergent needs which have left them unable to recover from the aftermath of the event. These aspirations seem to meld with their earlier aspirations of education for their children and a better quality of life. So the counter-aspirations seem to focus on returning to a state of normalcy which allows them to pursue their aspirations from before the event. Rather than an optimistic outlook about the future or a pessimistic outlook about the present, the aspirations seem to focus on the realities of their situation and a means to find a way out of it.

There are yearnings for their past lives, a desire for pre-event normalcy and the counter-aspirations are a means to address these yearnings but are based on the reality of their situation. In conclusion, counter-aspirations are representative of the struggles of the terror survivors and are the manifestation of their agency of resistance.

These findings are crucial to our understanding of the material-agency interface. These concepts do not exist in a vacuum or exclusive of each other; instead, they form a co-constitutive linkage. The denial of material rights leads to the emergence of an agency of resistance. The resistance fuelled by this agency is to fight for material rights and to ensure that the survivors' voices are heard loudly by everyone who will or will not listen. Essentially, the material reality experienced by survivors leads to a form of agency evolving from these experiences, which then serves to alter, resist or improve this material reality.

Distress experienced by survivors is not merely the result of the event itself but is shaped by the material realities resulting from these events. It is a complex web of interlinked events, perceptions and agencies that cause the distress of the event to persist long after its conclusion. This understanding is important as it allows for adequately addressing the needs of the survivors in the aftermath of a terror event. It is equally important to understand the complex range of emotions that emerge because of the current inadequacies in the systems formed to address the needs of survivors and how these result in the emergence of agency for resistance. This will allow an understanding of why survivors resist against their inadequate material realities and to acknowledge that agency does not manifest only through emotions and feelings associated with hope and resilience but through emotions and feelings regarded as "negative" such as anger and hopelessness.

Agency and material realities are co-constitutive, and this understanding is crucial to ensure that policies in the future are adequately designed to allow for survivors to express their agency in forms that are less distressing, rather than having to form an agency of resistance due to the inadequacies of the present systems, which are unjust and inadequate.

Disciplinary Divides and Its Implications for Therapeutic Processes in the Global South

This section engages with the historical evolution of the field of trauma and memory studies, with a special focus on therapeutic processes for healing. It illustrates the disciplinary divides, the resulting gaps in our understanding and the contribution of the book in bridging these gaps. This section brings forth the differences in the ontological and epistemological positions taken by the disciplines in engaging with trauma and memory, and its implications for healing, especially in the Global South. Research on trauma, memory and healing is approached from a wide range of disciplinary perspectives. This section, however, limits itself to the broad disciplinary contours in psychological, neurobiological and the socio-cultural studies to illustrate the historical emergence of therapeutic processes and their limitations, especially in the Global South. Drawing from the key contributions of the book in Chapters 3 and 4, this section concludes with the way forward in bridging some of the gaps in our current understanding and practice.

Psychological research on trauma and memory, especially the psychoanalytic and cognitive schools of thought, draws from the foundational work of scholars like William James, Janet Pierre and Sigmund Freud of the late 19th–early 20th century. The early work of these scholars (Janet, 1887; Freud, 1922; James, et al., 1890) brings forth the interlinkages between trauma, memory, the psychological mechanisms involved (repression and dissociation) and the resulting psychological disturbances (hysteria and obsessive behaviour).

These scholars not only postulated the interconnections but also contributed to elaborating the pathologies of trauma memory and ways of addressing it. James et al., (1890) conceptualized memory as dynamic and ever-changing, influenced by external and internal processes such as current needs, emotional states and experiences. Thus, memory was understood to be subjective and reconstructed by the interplay of consciousness, attention and personal experiences, laying the foundation for future research on the nature of memory and its malleability. Though James et al., (1890) emphasized both the external and internal processes, and the dynamic nature of memory, psychological research that followed, primarily focused on the time-invariant internal processes. Thus, these early scholars laid the foundation for the understanding of traumatic memory as a pathological process to be fixed through various therapeutic processes. This ontological position informed most psychological research and therapeutic interventions that have followed to date.

The post-World War I and World War II context and the work among veterans on shell shock, dissociation and fragmentation of trauma memory (Mott, 1919; Wittkower & Spillane, 1940; Finner, 1946; Glass, 1958) furthered the above understanding significantly. The understanding of the imperfect nature of memory that could be distorted or altered over time developed further within the field of traumatic memory studies. It focused on the malleability and reconstructed nature of memory, its implications for psychological distress and how to address it through therapeutic processes (Loftus & Palmer, 1974, Loftus, 1997). These research studies further opened the possibility of fixing pathological memories through therapeutic processes that focused on processing traumatic memories. The post-war context, the veteran psychological health issues and the possibilities of processing traumatic memories contributed to the consolidation of the diagnostic category of Post-Traumatic Stress Disorder in the *Diagnostic and Statistical Manual of Mental Disorders* (DSM-III) in the 1980s and its furtherance.

The professional recognition of PTSD led to the emergence of new therapeutic approaches and the re-emergence of certain traditional approaches of the mid-20th century and later, such as Supportive Counselling, Cognitive Behavioural Therapy (CBT), Family Therapy, Dialectical Behaviour Therapy (DBT) and Psychopharmacology, especially SSRIs (Selective Serotonin Reuptake Inhibitors) for the treatment of trauma in the 1990s. This period also witnessed several research studies exploring the mechanisms of memory distortion and processing, as well as the efficacy of various therapeutic processes. The therapeutic processes targeted the mechanisms of memory distortion and processing, in the treatment of PTSD and related psychological issues including that of anxiety and depression. Therapeutic processes such as cognitive behaviour therapy (Wright & Beck, 1983) and Eye Movement Desensitization and Reprocessing – EMDR (Shapiro & Forrest, 1997), were specifically identified for their effectiveness in the treatment of PTSD and other psychological sequelae.

Since the 1990s, brain research has also gained prominence focusing more on the biological brain structures and stress hormones to further the understanding of the impact of trauma on memory formation, retrieval and processing (Baum & Grunberg, 1995; Yehuda, 1998, 2000; Wang et al., 1995). This resulted in some of the recent advances in the use of neuroscientific tools such as neuroimaging and psychological assessments, facilitating a more accurate delineation of the effects of trauma on memory and evidence-informed treatment (Bremner, 1998; Rauch et al., 1998). The continued research on the malleability of memory (Nader, 2003; Loftus, 2003), gave new possibilities for understanding, processing and altering trauma-related memories. The malleability research emphasized the need for strategies to reduce subjective bias in memory research that rely less on narratives and more on neuroimaging and psychological assessments. These were some epistemological turns that emerged from the developments in neurobiological studies of the 1990s, in line with the ontological position that conceptualizes traumatic memories as a pathological process that contributes to pathologies of the mind.

The 1990s and early 2000s witnessed the emergence/re-emergence of specific neurobiology-informed therapies, like the Trauma-focused cognitive behavioural therapy, Eye Movement Desensitization and Reprocessing (EMDR), Somatic Experiencing, Polyvagal Theory-based Therapy, Cognitive Processing Therapy (CPT), Neuro-Affective Relational Model (NARM) and Brain spotting among others (Marcus et al., 1997; Zettl, 1998; Ogden & Minton, 2000; Vasquez, 2025; Hildebrand et al., 2017). These therapies build upon the neurobiological concepts of utilizing neuroplasticity, bilateral stimulation, autonomic nervous system regulation, especially the vagus nerve, addressing early attachment disruption and activating specific neural networks, among others.

The 2000s witnessed the re/emergence of several therapies of the past under the broader umbrella of trauma-informed care practices that emphasized safety and understanding within therapeutic settings such as the Attachment-Based Therapies, Mindfulness-Based Stress Reduction, Cognitive Behavioural Conjoint Therapy and Transformational Breath Work, among others (Steelman, 2019; Polusny et al., 2015; Monson et al., 2008; Bray, 2018). However, all these therapies were limited in terms of their long-term evidence base for effectiveness, understanding of how they worked, oversimplification, high levels of technical sophistication and mechanical approach. The most pertinent limitation emerging from the research findings of this book is the individualistic interventions that ignore the collective nature of trauma, limited availability and access to such interventions even in the Mumbai context and not understanding and addressing traumatic memory and stress from a holistic perspective that goes beyond biological dysregulation and restructuring maladaptive thought patterns. Socio-cultural studies have historically engaged with some of these concerns, and the review that follows identifies the broad range of socio-cultural dimensions explored in relation to trauma and memory, the therapeutic value of some of these dimensions and their implications for personal and felt experiences.

The social science research on trauma and memory, especially collective memory, illuminates its interlinkages with group/social identity, social cohesion, storytelling, social interaction and malleability, collectivist and individualist cultures and technology, among others (Halbwachs, 2020; Goffman, 1949; Lowenthal, 2015; Connerton, 1989; Misztal, 2003; Schudson, 1995). The early days of social science research stopped at the level of group or collective experiences and did not engage with the felt experiences of distress and recovery, especially those of individual survivors. The Holocaust and memorial studies have contributed in this regard by engaging with the social context of trauma along with the therapeutic value of narratives and memorials. The section that follows summarizes some of these key contributions of socio-cultural studies to illustrate how the book draws from and furthers the social science contributions to the understanding of distress and recovery.

The post-war memorials in the early 20th century marked the phase of recognition of psychological distress among survivors and affected communities. The mid-20th century post-World War II and Holocaust studies expanded the scope of research on trauma, memory and memorialization. Cultural memory studies (Halbwachs, 2020) lay the groundwork for the social framework of memory studies. The social framework emphasized the significance of the social context of trauma and memory, the contribution of memorials in shaping societal narratives of trauma and loss and its implications for collective memory.

Memorials were analysed to understand the societal struggles over memory, identity, historical interpretation and representation. The analysis focused on: the events; figures; the extent of public participation in the design and creation of memorials' dominant narratives; recognition, legitimation, shared histories and identities that they shape; diversity of narrative; conflicts with current value systems; and how they adapt to reflect current understanding of history and representation (Young, 1994; Caruth, 1996; Sennett, 1977; Rothberg, 2009; Schneider, 2011; Braun, 1994; Doss, 2012). The subset of research on memorials, representation and identity formation, focused on a range of inclusion-related issues starting with the representation of cultural and national identity that shapes memories of shared histories, to that of marginalized local voices of specific communities and groups (ethnic, religious and gender minorities, women) (Halbwachs, 2020; Hirsch, 2008). A subset of Holocaust studies specifically took forward the question of the social context of trauma and the significance of historical atrocities in shaping the psychological health of collectives and individuals. This subset focuses on the impact of memorial attributes, especially diversity, inclusion and representation, on collective memory, validation of trauma and loss, psychological well-being of marginalized groups and community resilience (Halbwachs, 2020; Young, 1994; Caruth, 1996; Sennett, 1977; Rothberg, 2009). Most of the above memorial studies are conceived within the frame of understanding trauma and its linkages to the various dimensions of memorialization. The dimensions focused upon were: the collective nature of memorials; complexities of memorialization; role of memorials in fostering collective remembrance; community engagement and reflection; representation and inclusion in memorials; memorialization of multidirectional memory; politics of commemoration; and the comparison of historical and contemporary memorial practices. Thus, these research studies illuminate the implications of exclusion from memorialization for psychological well-being and the counter memorialization processes of excluded groups and communities. But they do not illustrate the implications of this exclusion for individuals, especially the interface with the recovery trajectories.

The influence of neurobiological advancements of the 1990s was evident in memorial studies too. The interdisciplinary neurobiological research on the therapeutic significance of memorials illustrates the involvement of the amygdala, prefrontal cortex, neural circuits related to reward and satisfaction, neural pathways and neuroplastic changes among others, that facilitate emotional processing and regulation, and enhanced feelings of control, predictability, community and support. The potential of memorials to trigger strong emotional memories, enable social interactions, facilitate structured rituals and expression of grief, create new meaning and a narrative of loss, was identified to be the likely pathways that involved the above neurobiological processes facilitating enhanced coping mechanisms and recovery (LeDoux & Muller, 1997; Cacioppo & Patrick, 2008; Cohen, et al., 1996; Davidson & McEwen, 2012; Neimeyer, 2011, 2016).

Until the 21st century, most socio-cultural studies were primarily focused on collective memory, identity and representation and only made broad overarching references to psychological health implications among marginal groups and collectives. However, after the onslaught of PTSD and the proliferation of trauma-centric individual therapies since the 1980s, the social science discourse on trauma and memory makes a turnaround in the 21st century. Since the 2010s, the recent research studies that explore the therapeutic value of memorials (as listed in Chapter 4 introductory section) reinvent the social context discourse in relation to the lived experiences of certain sub-groups and their psychological health implications for larger collectives (felt experiences). The research studies on the therapeutic value of memorials focus on a range of topics encompassing neurobiology to cultural rituals that contribute to the healing process (Arel, 2018; Manderson, 2008; Caruth, 1996; Wagoner & de Luna, 2021; Schaff, 2018; Torres & Garcia-Hernandez, 2016).

Twenty-first century socio-cultural studies also focused on the possibility of artistic expression and digital memorials in challenging the power dynamics and politics of representation and commemoration, inherent in memorialization and their contribution to the inclusion of diverse marginalized voices (Schneider, 2011; Hebert, 2008; Hess, 2007).

As the above review demonstrates, the socio-cultural studies have made significant contributions to the understanding of trauma and memory and its implications for psychosocial health and recovery. Though both psychological and socio-cultural studies exploring the therapeutic possibilities branch out from the same foundations laid by Freud's work on the significance of memory and mourning (Freud, 1917), they ground themselves in very different ontological and epistemological positions and thus have differential implications for the field of mainstream mental health practice. The socio-cultural studies of trauma and memory engage with a wide range of social context dimensions and highlight their implications for psychosocial health of marginalized groups and collectives. They emphasize the following: the significance of the dynamic social and cultural context within which traumatic events occur, the non-linear notion of traumatic memory diverging from the pre-event, event and post-event linear temporality, the non-individualistic nature of trauma responses, the co-constituted nature of collective (official/public/counter-memory) and personal memory and the co-constitutive nature of mind and the world, diverging from the ontological dualism of Descartes (Bracken, 2002). It enables the re-conceptualization of trauma memory known to be fallible/distorted/disrupted/disjointed/repetitive/intrusive, as co-constituted, dynamic and temporally emerging in a non-linear fashion. However, this social science research only brings out the nuanced interface between memory, social context and personal experiences, and does not engage squarely with felt experiences as in the psychological discipline. In Chapter 4, the book extends this understanding from personal experiences to that of the felt experiences of terror survivors over the years and makes a humble attempt to bridge the gap between disciplinarily boxed research on trauma, memory and terrorism studies, towards a better understanding of human well-being and recovery. The book draws heavily from these alternative ontological and epistemological positions of trauma and memory, located within the historical, political and societal context of the past, present and future. By focusing on both the lived and felt experiences of survivors, the book takes forward the contributions of the socio-cultural studies in comprehensively understanding and addressing the psychosocial health and recovery of terror survivors.

In addressing psychosocial health, the psychological and neurobiological studies have had a very narrow focus on internal psychological and biological mechanisms contributing to psychopathology and those involved in addressing it. Though the socio-cultural studies have explored a wide range of socio-cultural factors impacting trauma, memory and recovery, and have given way to non-individualistic approaches, they too have been largely event, memorial and individual centric when it comes to exploring the therapeutic significance of memorials. As the book illustrates (Chapter 3), memorials and participation in memorialization are rare occurrence in the Global South. Often, the exclusion from the memorialization process contributes to more agony and pain, especially when one is still struggling to recover. Thus, the book illustrates alternative intervention strategies that are not event and memorial-centric, as identified by terror survivors.

Despite the contributions of memorial and Holocaust studies following the post-World War period, psychological and neurobiological research on trauma and memory resulted in the consolidation of PTSD as a diagnostic category within the DSM and was widely extended to explain, label and treat individual reactions to trauma in the form of several therapies and trauma-informed care practices. Though the trauma theories of the 1990s (like that of Caruth, 1996) dealt with the intersections of trauma, memory and representation, those that emphasized on trauma recovery and therapeutic processes (like that of Herman, 1992) dominated the mental health field of practice. The recognition of the social context of trauma and its societal implications for collective memory and identity formation continued to remain at the margins.

The cultural turn of the 2010s, with the renewed focus on the recognition of the historical, political and social context of trauma in shaping the lived experiences of certain sub-groups of society and the mental health implications for larger collectives (felt experiences), reinvents the social context discourse within the trauma, memory and memorialization research (Arel, 2018; Manderson, 2008; Caruth, 1996; Wagoner & de Luna, 2021; Schaff, 2018; Torres & Garcia-Hernandez, 2016). However, it makes limited linkages to the mainstream therapeutic processes or mental health practice with individuals. The few 21st-century contemporary studies on mental health and memorialization that focus on the possibilities of online memorials, memorials as therapeutic spaces, the process of creating localized community-based memorials as spaces of healing, representations of marginalized voices in memorialization and memorialization across cultural contexts, among others too are also limited with regard to their event- and memorial-centric approaches (Walter, 2015; McMillen et al., 2017; Mwaura, 2011; Henihan & Langness, 2019). Moreover, the therapeutic value of memorials is approached from the perspectives of larger collectives (collective memory and collective distress) and is not extended to explain and intervene with individual distress. Thus, the research and interventions emerging from memorial and Holocaust studies, which focus on the historical, political and social context of trauma, focus on collective memory. On the contrary, the psychological and neurobiological research on the therapeutic value of memorials focuses primarily on individual traumatic memory that is fragmented, distorted, dissociated, intrusive etc., and needs to be fixed. The interface between the collective and individual processes related to memory and distress is not explicitly explored. In addressing some of these research gaps, the book draws from the above 21st-century contemporary perspectives and extends them further to understand the marginalization and distress experienced and felt by the individual civilian survivors of 26/11. Thus, Chapter 3 goes beyond traumatic memory and engages with different categories of 26/11 remembering, the nature of representation and resulting identities. Chapter 4 connects the implications of these societal narratives to the individual survivors' lived and felt experiences over a period of

10 years, integrating time beyond being just a contextual factor. The chapter also illustrates the psychosocial processes that unfold with time, differently shaping the recovery trajectories among civilian survivors. Chapter 4 also illustrates the differential recovery trajectories that survivors take in a context with limited access to specialized traumatic stress-focused therapies, limited supportive services and memorials. These personal recovery trajectories are shaped by counter-narratives of memory, hope and aspirations.

Key Learnings from the Lived and Felt Experiences of Survivors and Way Forward

In conclusion, this section highlights the key learnings from the lived and felt experiences of survivors to chart the way forward for context-specific holistic recovery support services. The key learnings align with past research and move forward in illustrating the need for holistic recovery support services in the Global South, plagued with concerns of resource crunch and access issues. As illustrated by Nora (1996), Chapter 4 too illustrates how counter-memory and aspirations challenge the official memory that structures not just the memorials but also the victim identity, by bringing forth the multiplicity of personal identities that the survivors negotiate. The multiplicity of personal identity results in counter-aspirations that shift away from one's well-being to that of the next generation's well-being, to be secured through education and livelihood possibilities. This results in alternative personal recovery trajectories that are unique to each survivor and their social context. As in the work of Rothberg (2009), the book also illustrates how historical traumas reflected in marginal identities (of migrants and Muslim survivors) are relived in the post-26/11 recovery context, primarily as an outcome of neglect and abandonment of their aspirations and hopes, by the collective narrative shaped by official memory and memorials that followed. Some of these sub-groups attributed their neglect to their marginal identities of the past and struggled hard to dissociate themselves from the demonized identities of the terrorist reinforced by the official and public memory. The statements of sovereignty and condemnation of acts of terrorism in the immediate aftermath further strengthened the official narrative of nationalism and the threat to its integrity and security. As postulated by Misztal (2003) the social context of historical divides between the involved nations easily lends itself to an official/collective memory of threat to sovereignty and security concerns, which also gels well with public sentiments and thus targets a much larger audience, at the cost of neglecting the survivors and their real sufferings. A similar swing towards national security and the threat to sovereignty co-opted the survivor narratives in the initial phase of the post-event context and was later forgotten, marginalizing the survivors and their real sufferings. Chapter 4 illustrates the implications of this co-option and marginalization for the survivors' recovery and distress in the long run.

The memorial at Chabad House attempts to capture the Jewish way of life and the assault on Israeli identity. It further demonstrates cultural politics in memorialization from beyond the borders, like the observations of Assman & Conrad (2010). Assman & Conrad (2010) highlights how globalization shapes the transnational memory practices, where global cultural flows shape remembrance, bringing forth the significance of identity and cultural politics in memorialization. However, the Chabad House also remains the only memorial that includes the civilian survivors, challenging the official memory that the other memorials tend to align with. Thus, the role of global forces in the constitution of collective memory, by negating official memory and reconfiguring counter-memory, is evident in this analysis too. Chapter 4 also brings out the contradictions between official accounts of the response to the event and the fragmented, personal narratives of survivors, as highlighted by Caruth (1996). Chow (2014) examines the potential of counter-memory to challenge official narratives, especially in a context of political repression in authoritarian regimes. The current study demonstrates similar contradictions between official and counter-memory even within one of the world's largest democratic states.

In Chapter 3, the literature on the social framework of memory, memorials and trauma identifies different categories of remembering: official, collective and counter-memory. This literature reveals the complex range of societal factors that interact, compete and constitute public narrative and memory of a particular event. However, in the context of centrifugal disasters such as terror attacks, the affected community is spread across the country and beyond; thus, the possibility of the affected community's memories shaping public/collective memory of the attack is minimal. Therefore, the book makes a significant contribution in documenting the research that captures the official and public memory along with the counter-memory of the attack emerging from the lived and felt experiences of terror survivors.

The research literature on the role of memory in shaping identity (Halbwachs, 2020; Hirsch, 2008) brings forth several dimensions of significance to understand the emergence of victim and survivor identity in the post-terror attack context. Past research focuses on both individual and collective memory in relation to identity formation. The centrifugal nature of the attack impedes the possibility of the formation of a collective survivor identity among the affected individuals, as they do not share or inhabit the same community in the sense of geographic boundaries, knowing and meeting each other very rarely, as they are dispersed across the country and beyond. The collective memory that thus gets consolidated is among the public that vicariously witnessed the attack and its reportage. As the collective memory of survivors fails to consolidate, the official memory primarily determines the public memory of the event, and thus the victim identity prevails in both the official and public memory. The resulting neglect and abandonment of the survivors in the fight for justice lead to the emergence of counter-memory, which re-constitutes the survivor identity based on the counter-narratives of memory, hope and aspiration. However, this remains more at the personal level as forums for aggregating the same into collective counter-memory are minimal within the existing socio-political systems and structures. Thus, Chapter 4 is of significance in documenting these personal counter-narratives and the converging themes to inform future policy and action.

In Chapters 3 and 4, the book captures the various categories of memories emerging in the aftermath of the 26/11 Mumbai terror attack to understand the differential recovery processes experienced by survivors ten years after the attack. The official memory, aspirations and hope structure the victim identity and utilize the same as mere statistics in the fight for justice against the assault on national sovereignty and security. Thus, it dehumanizes the affected community by ignoring their humanity and recovery support needs after the terror attack. Chapter 3 captures the physical and symbolic remembering that followed immediately after the event and during the ten years of anniversary commemoration, to illustrate how the memorials are fragmented in terms of different victim identities, largely neglecting the civilians and the survivors altogether. The physical representation of civilian survivors, evident in the events organized to commemorate the attack, got reduced to tokenism as years passed by. The fight for justice, however, did not have any representation of the survivors and their recovery support needs, beyond the official narrative of national sovereignty and security. This abandonment and neglect led to the emergence of counter narratives (memory, hope and aspirations) as captured in Chapter 4. The emergence of counter narratives also entails the emergence of a survivor identity, rights claims and questions of differential treatment regarding healthcare, ex gratia and support services that marginalize a particular section of the survivors and challenge their status as citizens. Based on their lived and felt experiences of neglect and abandonment, they challenge and reinterpret the official narrative that fosters the understanding of differential personal recovery trajectories of the survivors. We problematize the hope and resilience-based approaches in terms of the responsibility for recovery being laid on the survivors, as it is no different from what unfolds in the current study and is likely to be the reality in most instances. Thus, the study makes a case for more proactive supportive interventions in the recovery context that address the material-immaterial world interlinkages in shaping well-being. As the above discussion section on disciplinary boundaries and its implications for therapeutic processes illuminates, the current dominant theoretical perspectives are limited in understanding and addressing the survivors' distress due to their cognitive, individualistic, event or memorial centredness. The emerging theoretical school of thought on situated cognition and affectivity since the 2000s (Stephan & Walter, 2020; Walter & Stephan 2023; Smith & Semin, 2004) relates better to the need to bridge the mind vs world dualism, as it attempts to link cognition, affect, emotion, body and the environment within its broad umbrella. As it is still an emerging theoretical perspective, the debates around its ontological position that aligns with that of the current study are many. The book makes a conscious choice to stay away from some of these core philosophical debates, drawing from the pragmatic worldview that the book grounds itself in. The book identifies the situated cognitions and emotions theoretical perspective as one of the ways forward, based on its alignment with the counter-narratives of the survivors. As it is an emerging theoretical school of thought, not much of its influence in the true sense is visible in the world of therapies. The limited therapeutic processes linked to or co-opting this theoretical perspective, such as the Ecologically Based Therapies, Social Cognitive Therapies, Narrative Exposure Therapy, Embodied Cognition Approaches and Situational Awareness and CBT, too get pulled into the trap of being cognitive, individualistic and event-centric. Probably an alternative to the label of therapeutic processes would be required to break free praxis from the clutches of curative processes. More attention, especially from social science researchers, is needed to evolve praxis that breaks off from these traps in addressing the dualism between mind and the world that dominates current therapeutic practices. This would be in line with the argument for taking the materiality of survivors' everyday lives (including the living physical body, animate objects and the material things in the survivors' environment) more seriously in understanding differential recovery trajectories and distress among survivors. The supportive services prioritized in the immediate aftermath of a disaster or emergency, in the form of psychosocial first aid (at least in theory if not in practice), if extended to the recovery phase, could be a humble starting point for an alternative approach that attempts to bridge the dualism of mind and the world in the recovery context. However, one must be cognizant of the heavy co-option of PFA by the traumatic stress perspective and build it further at a more systemic level, far from the clutches of individual therapeutic processes. The AAPTI model documents (Joseph & Jaswal, 2023) such an experiment. Originally conceptualized as a counselling centre, the AAPTI field office was shaped into a psychosocial support centre through reflexive praxis that squarely grounded itself around the lived and felt experiences of the survivors. The AAPTI field office comprehensively addressed both the pragmatic support and therapeutic needs of terror survivors in the long-term recovery context. The challenges faced by individuals and groups, pushed for the expansion of support services ranging from monthly sustenance, pensions, health, education, skills training, job placements, counselling and entrepreneurship support under the larger umbrella of psychosocial support services. Departing from the usual focus on the deceased or the injured, the interventions took the family (including the extended family dependent on the deceased and injured) and the immediate social context as the unit to be targeted. Thus, the intervention's focus went beyond bodily processes (death and injury) to address the social and political processes, through which trauma disrupts and detaches the body/mind from the world around. Taking cues from the survivors' rights claim, and the subsequent responses to other centrifugal disasters that did not elicit the kind of private material support that 26/11 did, the need for state leadership became evident. The negligible legal and institutional framework for long-term support that left the survivors in a state of abandonment without reprieve, further highlighted the need for giving voice to survivors, their plight and agency. However, the multiple failed efforts to build or strengthen collectives among the survivors illustrated the constraints inherent in centrifugal disasters and the material realities that bounded the agency of survivors. After 15 years of its initiation and constant negotiation with the state actors in the context of centrifugal disasters, the AAPTI model received the kind of state leadership and ownership in the response to the 2 June 2023 Balasore Train Disaster, India. Bihar State Disaster Management Authority from Bihar, India led the initiative of extending the AAPTI model of long-term recovery support to the train disaster survivors. The initiative over two years was successful in gaining state commitment and extended greater access to ex gratia, social welfare and livelihood support to survivors. With the engagement of the state missionary, the constraints of responding to survivors spread across the state were addressed in a very time efficient manner. However, issues of interdepartmental coordination, commitment and capacity were hampering uniform delivery of services to all survivors. The resource constraints manifested in terms of stringent eligibility criteria and yearly budgetary allocations of regular welfare and developmental initiatives that are unable to accommodate the extra demands of disasters, further illustrated the material realities that constrain both agency and recovery support services. The breakthrough in state leadership and the efforts to address the gaps in policy and institutional framework will have to be built further. The shift in focus from event, individual and sectoral centric interventions to that of survivor focused interventions that are inclusive of their family and immediate social context, needs further reinforcement. Above all the alternative conceptualization of psychosocial distress and comprehensive intervention strategies will have to be pushed further to gain the confidence of professionals and bureaucrats in the Global South, to consider these extended supportive services as a pragmatic solution to addressing the recovery needs and distress of survivors. This book is a humble contribution towards the same.

References

AG vs Shiv Kumar Yadav And Anr. (2015). AIR 2015 SUPREME COURT 3501. Supreme Court of India. https://indiankanoon.org/doc/33982557/. Accessed May 8, 2025.

Agamben, G., & Hiepko, A. (2002). *Homo sacer* (p. 6). Suhrkamp.

Arel, S. (2018). The power of place: Trauma recovery and memorialization. *Stellenbosch Theological Journal*, *4*(2), 15–32.

Assmann, A., & Conrad, S. (Eds.). (2010). *Memory in a global age*. Basingstoke: Palgrave Macmillan.

Bajpai, G. S. (Ed.). (1997). *Victim in the criminal justice process: Perspective on police and judiciary*. Uppal Publishing House.

Baum, A. A. G. N., & Grunberg, N. (1995). Measurement of stress hormones. *Measuring Stress: A Guide for Health and Social Scientists*, 175–192.

Bracken, P. (2002). *Trauma: Culture, meaning and philosophy*. Whurr Publishers.

Braun, R. (1994). The Holocaust and problems of historical representation. *History and Theory*, 172–197.

Bray, P. (2018). Holotropic Breathwork as a therapeutic intervention for survivors of trauma: an autoethnographic case study. *In What Happened? Re-presenting Traumas, Uncovering Recoveries* (pp. 187-218). Brill.

Bremner, J. D. (1998). Neuroimaging of posttraumatic stress disorder. *Psychiatric Annals*, *28*(8), 445–450.

Cacioppo, J. T., & Patrick, W. (2008). *Loneliness: Human nature and the need for social connection*. WW Norton & Company.

Caruth, C. (1996). *Unclaimed experience: Trauma, narrative, and history*. John Hopkins University Press. Available at: http://ereserve.library.utah.edu/Annual/ECS/6950/Thompson/caruth.pdf. Accessed April 14, 2025.

Chow, R. (2014). Not like a native speaker: On languaging as a postcolonial experience. New York, Columbia University Press.

Cohen, D., Nisbett, R. E., Bowdle, B. F., & Schwarz, N. (1996). Insult, aggression, and the southern culture of honor: An "experimental ethnography." *Journal of personality and social psychology*, *70*(5), 945.

Connerton, P. (1989). *How societies remember*. Cambridge University Press.

Davidson, R. J., & McEwen, B. S. (2012). Social influences on neuroplasticity: Stress and interventions to promote well-being. *Nature Neuroscience*, *15*(5), 689–695.

Doss, E. (2012). *Memorial mania: Public feeling in America*. University of Chicago Press.

Farber, S. (2024). Trauma, truth, and testimony: analysing terrorism survivors' victim impact statements. *International Journal of Comparative and Applied Criminal Justice*, 1–19.

Farber, S., & Benichou, N. (2021). Between victims of crime and victims of terrorism: Victims' rights in the military courts in the west bank. *New Criminal Law Review*, *24*(4), 568–600.

Finner, R. W. (1946). Psychiatry in World War II. *Journal of the American Medical Association*, *132*(16), 1034–1034.

Freud, S. (1917). Mourning and melancholia. *The Standard Edition of the Complete Psychological Works of Sigmund Freud*, *14*(1914–1916), 237–258.

Freud, S. (1922). Repression. *The Psychoanalytic Review*, *9*(1913-1957), 444.

Garcia Gonzalez, A. (2019). *Multiple violences and practices of peace: A feminist approach to the post-ceasefire process in the Basque Country* (Doctoral dissertation, University of Brighton).

Goffman, E. (1949). Presentation of self in everyday life. *American Journal of Sociology*, *55*(1), 6–7.

Halbwachs, M. (2020). *The collective memory*. University of Chicago Press. (Original Work Published in 1950) Available at: https://d1wqtxts1xzle7.cloudfront.net/9579216/hawlbachsspace-libre.pdf?1390857178=&response-content-disposit

ion=inline%3B+filename%3DHalbwachs_Coser_On_Collective_Memory.pdf&Expires=1746176425&Signature=cKlGNuE1Bim3lJRHKX4Jldl1Qoclk20Wz7si2kdDC6diH~RgMAbTlXDNOcFKh-cKKit2hUu-NLz9q34UIsm1Mk9bL2nFAXLImzw6RyAJXQAMZgVJZFq4UCiwKDp2WfwSSODfusaMNtJJnY7T990sIKiaoFLiwH0Fm0mtB8~HjG1Lds0xsW-jBHeOwUMcdppCILPFoU4VkiSrUpngJcdPwOS4CoXkno3VzeH6KrRrbS2l0Je9vb3ErMtLzoajZ4f~AlnGG3WPZglkHLJt0DYqvkSMb3FB0VMCsi8PNC8~KmLL7v0mUS9mgEmSEVEFlMFa3GRHPB7rz7ratzARpGIOVw__&Key-Pair-Id=APKAJLOHF5GGSLRBV4ZA. Accessed May 2, 2025

Hebert, S. (2008). *Digital memorialization: Collective memory, tragedy, and participatory spaces*. University of Denver.

Henihan, A., & Langness, M. (2019). Memorials matter: On the role of memorials in manipulating space to create places of racial reckoning. *Journey*, *3*, 25–34.

Herman, J. L. (1992). Trauma and recovery Judith Lewis Herman, MD.

Hess, A. (2007). In digital remembrance: Vernacular memory and the rhetorical construction of web memorials. *Media, Culture & Society*, *29*(5), 812–830.

Hildebrand, A., Grand, D., & Stemmler, M. (2017). Brainspotting–the efficacy of a new therapy approach for the treatment of Posttraumatic Stress Disorder in comparison to Eye Movement Desensitization and Reprocessing. *Mediterranean Journal of Clinical Psychology*, *5*(1), Available at https://cab.unime.it/journals/index.php/MJCP/article/viewFile/1376/pdf_2, Accessed on 4th December 2025.

Hirsch, M. (2008). The generation of postmemory. *Poetics Today*, *29*(1), 103–128. https://scholar.princeton.edu/sites/default/files/jns/files/svia_2017_india_state_coin_histories.pdf

James, W., Burkhardt, F., Bowers, F., & Skrupskelis, K. (1890). *The principles of psychology* (Vol. 1, No. 2, pp. 315-329). London: Macmillan.

Janet, P. (1887). L'ANESTHÉSIE SYSTÉMATISÉE ET LA DISSOCIATION DES PHÉNOMÈNES PSYCHOLOGIQUES. *Revue Philosophique de La France et de l'Étranger*, *23*, 449–472. http://www.jstor.org/stable/41072829

Joseph, J., & Jaswal, S. (2023). *Centrifugal disasters: Trajectories of vulnerability, recovery and resilience*. Routledge India.

LeDoux, J. E., & Muller, J. (1997). Emotional memory and psychopathology. *Philosophical Transactions of the Royal Society of London. Series B: Biological Sciences*, *352*(1362), 1719–1726.

Lee, C. J. (2020). *The necropolitics of Covid-19. Africa is a country*. Available at https://africasacountry.com/2020/04/the-necropolitics-of-covid-19, Accessed on 4th December 2025.

Liebig, N. N. (2019). Trauma, embodiment, and compromised agency. *Public Philosophy Journal*, *2*(2), 1–8.

Loftus, E. F. (1997). Creating false memories. *ScientificAmerican*, *277*(3), 70-75.

Loftus, E. F. (2003). Make-believe memories. *American Psychologist*, *58*(11), 867.

Loftus, E. F., & Palmer, J. C. (1974). Reconstruction of automobile destruction: An example of the interaction between language and memory. *Journal of verbal learning and verbal behavior, 13*(5), 585-589.

Lowenthal, D. (2015). *The past is a foreign country–revisited*. Cambridge University Press, UK (Original Work Published in 1985).

Manderson, L. (2008). Acts of remembrance: The power of memorial and the healing of indigenous Australia. *Adler Museum Bulletin*, *34*(2), 5–19.

Marcus, S. V., Marquis, P., & Sakai, C. (1997). Controlled study of treatment of PTSD using EMDR in an HMO setting. *Psychotherapy: Theory, Research, Practice, Training*, *34*(3), 307.

Mbembe, A. (2006). Necropolitics. *Raisons Politiques*, *21*(1), 29–60.

MC Glass, C. A. J. (1958). Observations upon the epidemiology of mental illness in troops during warfare. In *Symposium on preventive and social psychiatry, sponsored jointly by the Walter Reed Army Institute of Research, Walter Reed Army Medical Center, and the National Research Council* (p. 185). U.S. Government Printing Office.

McMillen, H. L., Campbell, L. K., & Svendsen, E. S. (2017). 'The power of living things': Living memorials as therapeutic landscapes. *Medicine Anthropology Theory*, *4*(1).

Meher, S., & Shukla, G. (2017). The restorative justice to the victims of terrorist attacks in India. *Journal of the Indian Law Institute*, *59*(4), 383–396.

Ministry of Home Affairs. (2010). Revised guidelines of 'Central Scheme for Assistance to Civilians Victims/Family of Victims of Terrorist, Communal and Naxal Violence. https://www.mha.gov.in/sites/default/files/2022-09/T-Guide141008_2%5B1%5D.pdf. Accessed May 8, 2025.

Ministry of Home Affairs. (2019). *Revised guidelines of 'Central Scheme for Assistance to Civilian Victims/Family of Victims of Terrorist/Communal/ LWE Violence and Cross Border Firing and Mine/IED Blasts on Indian Territory*. https://www.mha.gov.in/sites/default/files/2023-01/GuidelinesoftheCentralSchemeforAssistancetoCivilianVictims_E_04112020%5B1%5D.PDF. Accessed May 8, 2025.

Misztal, B. (2003). *Theories of social remembering*. McGraw-Hill Education (UK).

Monson, C. M., Fredman, S. J., & Adair, K. C. (2008). Cognitive–behavioral conjoint therapy for posttraumatic stress disorder: Application to Operation Enduring and Iraqi Freedom veterans. *Journal of Clinical Psychology*, *64*(8), 958–971.

Mott, F. W. (1919). *War neuroses and shell shock*.

Mwaura, M. W. (2011). Community-based social healing approaches in South Africa: A case study of the Institute for Healing of Memories (Doctoral dissertation, University of the Western Cape).

Nader, K. (2003). Memory traces unbound. *Trends in Neurosciences*, *26*(2), 65–72.

Neimeyer, R. A. (2011). Reconstructing meaning in bereavement. *Handbook of Psychotherapy in Cancer Care*, 247–257.

Neimeyer, R. A. (2016). Meaning reconstruction in the wake of loss: Evolution of a research program. *Behaviour Change*, *33*(2), 65–79.

Nora, P. (1996). *Realms of memory: Rethinking the French past*. Columbia University Press.

Ogden, P., & Minton, K. (2000). Sensorimotor psychotherapy: One method for processing traumatic memory. *Traumatology*, *6*(3), 149–173.

Owens, P. (2009). Reclaiming 'bare life'?: Against Agamben on refugees. *International Relations*, *23*(4), 567–582.

Polusny, M. A., Erbes, C. R., Thuras, P., Moran, A., Lamberty, G. J., Collins, R. C., ... & Lim, K. O. (2015). Mindfulness-based stress reduction for posttraumatic stress disorder among veterans: A randomized clinical trial. *Jama*, *314*(5), 456–465.

Rajan, V. N. (1981). *Victimology in India: An introductory study*. Allied Publishers.

Rauch, S. L., Shin, L. M., Whalen, P. J., & Pitman, R. K. (1998). Neuroimaging and the neuroanatomy of posttraumatic stress disorder. *Cns Spectrums*, *3*(S2), 30–41.

Rothberg, M. (2009). Multidirectional memory and the universalization of the Holocaust. In *Remembering the Holocaust: A Debate*, 123–134.

Saraswati Parabhai & Anr. vs Grid Corporation of Orissa & Ors. (1999). AIR2000ORI13. Orissa High Court. https://indiankanoon.org/doc/1417282/. Accessed May 8, 2025

Sarwan Singh & Ors Etc vs State of Punjab. (1978). Air 1978 supreme court 1525. Supreme Court of India. https://indiankanoon.org/doc/285059/. Accessed May 8, 2025

Schaff, P. (2018). Collaborative commemoration: Narratives as transactional memorials to heal the wounds of War and Trauma. *Military Behavioral Health*, *6*(2), 127–133.

Schneider, R. (2011). *Performing remains: Art and war in times of theatrical reenactment*. Routledge.

Schudson, M. (1995). Dynamics of distortion in collective memory. *Memory Distortion: How Minds, Brains, and Societies Reconstruct the Past, 346*.

Sennett, R. (1977). *The fall of public man*. WW.

Shapiro, F., & Forrest, M. S. (1997). Healing the ravages of rape. EMDR eye movement desensitization & reprocessing: The breakthrough "eye movement" therapy for overcoming anxiety, stress and trauma. *Basic Books New York*, NY.

Sharpio, J. N., Eynde, O. V., Ingram, K., & Agawu, E. A. (2017). Indian State counterinsurgency policies: Brief historical summaries. *Empirical Studies of Conflict*.

Smith, E. R., & Semin, G. R. (2004). Socially situated cognition: Cognition in its social context. *Advances in Experimental Social Psychology*, *36*, 57–121.

Steelman, B. (2019). Attachment-based therapy for elder suffering PTSD symptoms: A narrative of modeling efficacy for improved outcomes. *Perspectives in Psychiatric Care*, *55*(1), 72–74.

Stephan, A., & Walter, S. (2020). Situated affectivity. In *The Routledge handbook of phenomenology of emotion* (pp. 299–311). Routledge.

The Prosecutor v. Dyilo. (2007). ICC-01/04-01/06. The International Criminal Court. https://www.icc-cpi.int/sites/default/files/CourtRecords/CR2007_02360.PDF. Accessed May 8, 2025.

Theisen-Womersley, G. (2021). *Trauma and resilience among displaced populations: A sociocultural exploration* (p. 305). Springer Nature.

Toribio Medina, M. (2024). 20 years on. A walk through the memorialisation of the 11M attacks. In: Karcher, K., Dimcheva, Y., Toribio Medina, M., Parkes, M. (Eds.), *Urban terrorism in contemporary Europe: Remembering, imagining and anticipating violence* (pp. 47–67). Springer International Publishing.

Torres, C., & García-Hernández, A. M. (2016). From violation to voice, from pain to protest: Healing and transforming unjust loss through the use of rituals and memorials. In: Køster, A. & Kofod, E. H. (Eds.), *Handbook of social justice in loss and grief* (pp. 202–212). Routledge.

Tota, A. L. (2005). Terrorism and collective memories: Comparing bologna, naples and madrid 11 March. *International Journal of Comparative Sociology*, *46*(1–2), 55–78.

United Nations. (1985, November 29). Declaration of basic principles of justice for victims of crime and abuse of power, UN, 40th Session, UN Doc A/RES/40/34., UN, 40th Session, UN Doc A/RES/40/34. https://www.unodc.org/pdf/rddb/CCPCJ/1985/A-RES-40-34.pdf. Accessed May 8, 2025.

United Nations. (2016, July 19), *The United Nations global counter-Terrorism strategy review*, UN, 70th Session, UN Doc A/RES/70/291. https://docs.un.org/en/A/RES/70/291. Accessed May 8, 2025.

United Nations. (2006, September 20), *The United Nations global counter-Terrorism strategy*, UN, 60th Session, UN Doc A/RES/60/288. https://docs.un.org/en/A/RES/60/288. Accessed May 8, 2025.

Vasquez, J. (2025). The impact of the Neuro Affective Relational Model (NARM) on client agency. *Studies in Clinical Social Work: Transforming Practice, Education and Research*, *95*(1), 1–20.

Ventevogel, P., Ryan, G. K., Kahi, V., & Kane, J. C. (2019). Capturing the essential: Revising the mental health categories in UNHCR's Refugee Health Information System. *Intervention Journal of Mental Health and Psychosocial Support in Conflict Affected Areas*, *17*(1), 13–22.

Vollmeyer, J. (2023). Materiality and the construction of cultural narratives of mass violence. *Journal of Perpetrator Research*, *5*, 107–118.

Wagoner, B., & de Luna, I. B. (2021). Collective grief: Mourning rituals, politics and memorial sites. In: Harris, D. L. & Bordere, T. C. (Eds.), *Cultural, existential and phenomenological dimensions of grief experience* (pp. 197–213). Routledge.

Walby, S. (2021). The COVID pandemic and social theory: Social democracy and public health in the crisis. *European Journal of Social Theory*, *24*(1), 22–43.

Walter, S., & Stephan, A. (2023). Situated affectivity and mind shaping: Lessons from social psychology. *Emotion Review*, *15*(1), 3–16.

Walter, T. (2015). New mourners, old mourners: Online memorial culture as a chapter in the history of mourning. *New Review of Hypermedia and Multimedia*, *21*(1–2), 10–24.

Wang, S., Mason, J., Southwick, S., Johnson, D., Lubin, H., & Charney, D. (1995). Relationships between thyroid hormones and symptoms in combat-related posttraumatic stress disorder. *Psychosomatic Medicine*, *57*(4), 398–402.

Wesley, D. (2024). Framing terrorism survivors: Visual representation of Boko Haram survivors in international news media. *Western Journal of Communication*, 1–22.

Wittkower, E., & Spillane, J. P. (1940). Neuroses in war—I. *British Medical Journal*, *1*(4127), 223.

Wright, J. H., & Beck, A. T. (1983). Cognitive therapy of depression: Theory and practice. *Psychiatric Services, 34*(12), 1119-1127.

Yanay, U., & Gal, T. (2010). Lobbying for rights. *International Handbook of Victimology*, 373–396.

Yehuda, R. (1998). Psycho-neuroendocrinology of post-traumatic stress disorder. *Psychiatric Clinics of North America*, *21*(2), 359–379.

Yehuda, R. (2000). Biology of posttraumatic stress disorder. *Journal of Clinical Psychiatry*, *61*, 14–21.

Young, J. E. (1994). The texture of memory: Holocaust memorials and meaning. Yale University Press.

Zettl, L. A. (1998). Knights in shining armor: A phenomenological exploration of the experience of trauma in emergency service personnel and the impact of Somatic Experiencing (RTM). Pacifica Graduate Institute.

Zimmermann, M. (2016). When psychological first aid is not enough: Personal reflections on psychosocial interventions in Duma, a village in North West Bank. *Intervention*, *14*(3), 200–206.

Index